目录 / TABLE OF CONTENT / INHALTSVERZEICHNIS

* Zu Gunsten der einfacheren Lesbarkeit wird im Folgenden sowohl für die männliche als auch für die weibliche Form die männliche Form verwendet.

中国新工人的形成
三十年流动的历史

THE MAKING OF
THE CHINESE NEW WORKING CLASS
THIRTY YEARS OF MIGRATION

Chinas neue Arbeiterklasse
Dreißig Jahre Wanderarbeit

Dear readers,
It is a great pleasure to share with you this publication, which accompanies *The Making of the Chinese New Working Class*, an exhibition by the Culture and Art Museum of Migrant Workers Beijing that took place at MINI / Goethe-Institut Curatorial Residencies Ludlow 38 in New York from July 14 through September 4, 2011.
The Culture and Art Museum of Migrant Workers (CAMMW) was initiated in 2008 by a former migrant worker and musician, Sun Heng, and is located in Picun, a village outside Beijing that is home to more than 10,000 migrant workers. CAMMW is a project of Migrant Workers' Home, an NGO founded in 2002, and dedicated to supporting the rights of migrant workers, providing education for their children, and serving as a community center. The purpose of the museum is to record the histories of migrant workers and to advocate for the value of their labor. The display *The Making of the Chinese New Working Class* travelled to New York after having been part of the exhibition *The Potosí Principle* at the Museu Reina Sofia in Madrid, the Haus der Kulturen der Welt and the IG Metall (metal workers union) in Berlin, and the Museo Nacional de Etnografía y Folklore in La Paz. Not unlike at these venues, it was presented here as an installation consisting of eight thematic topics that illustrate migrant workers' living conditions in the front gallery, and the re-creation of a migrant worker's living space in the rear gallery.
Materials such as working tools and identity cards donated by migrant workers from across China were on display. Photographs and artifacts such as music CD's and video DVD's portrayed the life in Picun village and the work of the Culture and Art Museum of Migrant Workers.

According to the Department of City Planning New York City has the largest Chinese population of any city outside of Asia[1]. The geographical location of Ludlow 38 in the heart of New York's Chinatown was one of the motivators in bringing this exhibit to the city. To coincide with the exhibition Ludlow 38 launched a series of side-events conceived in collaboration with New York-based artist Marty Kirchner and The Public School New York. With a street assembly and discussion, a performance, a symposium, and film screenings we attempted to examine the issues raised by the exhibition—reflecting a particular situation in China—and to locate them in relation to our context in New York:
During the exhibition opening on July 14, Zhibin Lin, research co-ordinator of The Culture and Art Museum of Migrant Workers participated in a public meeting with Ellen David Friedman, a union organizer and labor educator in the U.S. and China. Together they discussed the exhibition, Zhibin Lin's work in China, as well as the recent history of Chinese migrant labor, including internal migration to urban economic zones, and a new wave of proletarianization.
The next day New York-based artists Jason Boughton and Arlen Austin, performing as The Hanns Eisler Nail Salon / Nail Workers Chorus, joined Maria and Nancy at Unique Hairstylist on 47 Essex Street to present a new cabaret performance: *(re) Zoning, Manicured*, a music soiree that "described zoning policy as it currently exists on the Lower East Side and potential reforms that will help to preserve small businesses and affordable housing."
During the same weekend on July 16, 2011, together with Marty Kirchner we organized the Symposium *Precarious Power: Syndicalism, Solidarity, and the New Organizational Paradigm* at the Murphy Institute for Worker Education and Labor Studies in New York. Invited panelists were Immanuel Ness, Professor of Political Science at Brooklyn College, City University of New York; Jeff Becker, International Labor Rights Forum, Washington, DC; Daniel Gross, Industrial Workers of the World and Brandworkers International, New York; Carrie Gleason, Retail Action Project, New York and Not An Alternative, New York. With their kind permission we are presenting some of the panelists contributions in this volume.

The premiere of Marty Kirchner's new video *¡Ni un paso astrás!* (2011) and a screening of *Metropolis. Report from China* (2006) by Maya Schweizer and Clemens von Wedemeyer concluded the exhibition at Ludlow 38.

My very special thanks goes to Zhibin Lin for the generous dialogue she led with us during the project and for granting permission to reproduce parts of the (now out of print) publication originally developed for the *The Potosí Principle*. We have chosen to reproduce these parts in Chinese, English and German from the original publication in slightly edited form. I would also like to thank the graphic designers HIT, Spector Books in Leipzig and Mona Wischhoff who helped editing this publication. Our thanks goes to all the contributors to the project in New York and this publication. Without their generous collaboration a contextualization of *The Making of the Chinese New Working Class* for its presentation in New York would not have been possible. Furthermore I like to thank the partners of this project, Haus der Kulturen der Welt, Berlin and Kulturstiftung des Bundes. Finally I like to express my gratitude to the program directors of Goethe-Institut New York, Dr. Stephan Wackwitz and Wenzel Bilger as well as MINI and the Friends of Goethe for their continuing support of MINI / Goethe-Institut Curatorial Residencies Ludlow 38.

Tobi Maier, Curator
November 2011

1 An 1870 census shows there were only 23 Chinese living in New York City. But the numbers increased to 120 in 1872, 853 in 1880, 2,559 in 1890, and 6,321 in 1900 with more than half a million residing in the city in 2010 (Chinese Consolidated Benevolent Association).

COLOPHON

Editors: Tobi Maier and Mona Wischhoff
Organisation of events in New York: Marty Kirchner and Tobi Maier, with assistance from Justin Williams
Installation views at Ludlow 38, Photo: Mikolaj Szoska
Design: HIT
Publishers: Spector Books, Leipzig and MINI / Goethe-Institut Curatorial Residencies Ludlow 38, New York

Acknowledgements: all the contributors to this publication, Zhibin Lin, Sun Heng, Sonja Oehler and Haus der Kulturen der Welt Berlin, Alice Creischer, Andreas Siekmann, Max Jorge Hinderer, Matthijs de Bruijne, Marty Kirchner, Ellen David Friedman, The Public School New York, Maya Schweizer and Clemens von Wedemeyer, Camille Okhio, Anna Ostoya

MINI / Goethe-Institut Curatorial Residencies Ludlow 38 is supported by MINI and Friends of Goethe.

The Making of the Chinese New Working Class has been supported by Haus der Kulturen der Welt, Berlin and Kulturstiftung des Bundes.

The Goethe-Institut is the Federal Republic of Germany's cultural institution operational worldwide. We promote the study of German abroad and encourage international cultural exchange. We also foster knowledge about Germany by providing information on its culture, society and politics. With our network of Goethe-Instituts, Goethe Centres, cultural societies, reading rooms, and exam and language learning centres we have played a central role in the cultural and educational policies of Germany for over 50 years.

Published by: Spector Books
Harkortstraße 10, D-04107 Leipzig
+49 (0)341 212 24 11
mail@spectorbooks.com
www.spectorbooks.com

Printed in Germany

ISBN: 978-3-940064-42-4

KULTURSTIFTUNG DES BUNDES

GOETHE INSTITUT

MINI

HAUS DER KULTUREN DER WELT

中国新工人的形成—三十年流动的历史
The Making of the Chinese New Working Class—Thirty Years of Migration
Chinas neue Arbeiterklasse – Dreißig Jahre Wanderarbeit

1 前言

中国改革开放30年的历史，是中国工业化、城市化快速发展和经济腾飞的历史，推动这一历史进程的主力军是两亿多从农村流向城市的中国移民工人。他们不仅为中国经济的发展做出了巨大的历史贡献，同时也直接推动着世界经济的发展。中国改革开放30年的历史也是中国新工人群体正在形成的历史。工人阶级的形成并不是有新工人出现就自动完成的，是要通过经济、社会、制度、文化和新工人自身认同的综合作用才会出现、形成和发展的。新工人文化体现了打工群体对现实和自身地位的认识和反思，及对公平社会的渴求。就像玻利维亚油画承载着移民工人的记忆一样，我们的文化反映了我们的现实，这也将成为新工人形成过程的一种记忆。
各个国家和民族的发展历史不同，但是当我们探索发展规律的时候还是可以发现很多共性的东西。这些移民工人所受到来自资本和权力的压迫，从规律和本质上来讲，的确可以和过去殖民国家的资本和权力对殖民地人民的剥削和压迫进行类比。

1 Introduction

In the past thirty years since China first adopted reform policies, opening its doors to the world, the country has progressed extremely fast in areas of industrialization, urbanization, and economic development. The main reason for this development has been the two hundred million plus migrant workers who have played an indispensable role in the country's rise while also contributing greatly to the world economy. Over the course of this development a new working class has risen. However, the creation of a new working class is not necessarily contemporaneous with an emergence of new workers. Instead, it is a process of economic, societal, institutional and cultural transformation accompanied by the working class's own awareness raising and the reflection of their identity. The culture of this new working class reflects these workers' own recognition of their status as well as their desire for a more equal society. Just as Bolivian oil paintings carry the memory of migrant workers[1], Chinese migrant workers' culture reflects the realities of China's new workers and will eventually also become collective memory. The oppression that migrants face from the forces of capitalism is comparable to past colonial exploitation.

1 The bolivian oil paintings are mentioned here because of the original text context as part of *The Potosí Principle*.

1 Einleitung

Mit Einleitung der Reformpolitik vor 30 Jahren öffnete sich China der restlichen Welt und hat seitdem in den Bereichen Industrialisierung und Urbanisierung sowie in der wirtschaftlichen Entwicklung rasante Veränderungen erfahren. Mehr als 200 Millionen Wanderarbeiter machen den wirtschaftlichen Aufstieg Chinas im globalen Wettbewerb überhaupt erst möglich. Im Zuge dieser Entwicklung bildet sich eine neue Arbeiterklasse heraus, die nicht in erster Linie aus dem Anstieg der Anzahl der Arbeiter resultiert, sondern vielmehr auf einen Prozess wirtschaftlichen, gesellschaftlichen, institutionellen und kulturellen Wandels zurückzuführen ist, in dem das Bewusstsein für eine gemeinsame Identität als Klasse entsteht. In der Kultur dieser neuen Arbeiterklasse spiegelt sich sowohl der Wunsch nach einer gerechteren Gesellschaft als auch das eigene Statusbewusstsein wider. Ebenso wie bolivianische Ölgemälde die Geschichte dortiger Wanderarbeiter überliefern[1], reflektiert die Kultur der chinesischen Wanderarbeiter die Lebenswirklichkeit dieser neuen Arbeiterklasse und wird ins kollektive Gedächtnis Chinas eingehen. Auch wenn jede Nation ihre eigenen Grundgedanken verfolgt, finden sich bei genauerer Betrachtung der nationalen, historischen Entwicklungen auch allgemeingültige Prinzipien. Die Unterdrückung, der die Wanderarbeiter in China durch die vereinten Kräfte von Kapital und Macht ausgesetzt sind, ist vergleichbar mit der damaligen Ausbeutung während der Kolonialzeit.

1 Die bolivianischen Ölgemälde werden hier aufgrund des ursprünglichen Textzusammenhangs als Teil der Ausstellung *The Potosí Principle* genannt.

2 概况

2.1 谁是我们说的新工人群体

是指户籍身份是农民,但是已经离开农村不再从事农业生产，而是在城市生活和工作,通过付出自己的劳动以换取工资或劳务报酬的广大各行各业的劳动者.2009年3月25日中国统计局发布数据称，截至2008年底，中国移民工总数为2.25亿人。其中本乡镇以外就业的外出移民工数量为1.4亿人。国务院研究室在2006年4月发表的《中国农民工调研报告》显示，目前移民工这一新兴的工人阶级队伍在人数上已超过传统工人人数，成为当代中国工人阶级的主力军。例如，北京市吸纳全国400万流动人口（民间测算520万），占北京市常住人口的30%。

打工群体对中国和世界的贡献是以他们的低工资和几乎不享受社会福利为代价的。国家统计局服务业调查中心在2006年10月发布的农民工生活质量调查显示,打工者的平均月收入为966元。2009年9月人力资源和社会保障部公布，移民工月平均工资水平在1400块钱左右。北京工友之家在2009年的调查显示,苏州工人的月工资在金融危机前为1987元,金融危机后为1402元;深圳工友月工资金融危机前为1476元,金融危机后为1258元。

根据国家统计局服务业调查中心在2006年10月的移民工调查显示，男性占 65%,女性占35%。深圳市人事局2006年进行的调查显示,在深圳的移民工中女性比例较高，男性占48%，女性占52%。

Areas of employment of migrant workers /
Beschäftigungsbereiche von Wanderarbeitern

38% 制造业 / Manufacturing / Industrielle Produktion
18% 建筑业 / Construction / Baugewerbe
12% 服务业 / Services / Dienstleistung
8% 住宿和餐饮行业 / Accommodation and Catering / Hotelerie
8% 批发和零售贸易业 / Wholesale and Retail / Groß- und Einzelhandel
6% 交通运输、仓储和邮政业 / Logistics / Logistik
10% 其他 / Other / Andere

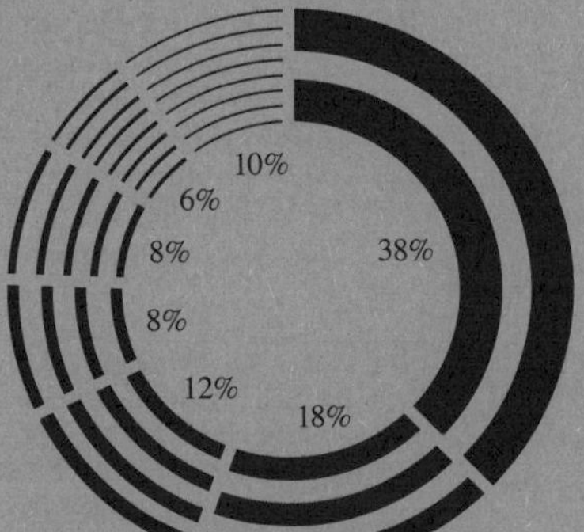

Source: The National Bureau of Statistics, September 2009 /
Quelle: Das Nationale Amt für Statistik, September 2009

2 Overview

2.1 Who are the new workers?

"The new workers" refers to the workers who have the registration status of a peasant, but have left the countryside and abandoned agricultural production in order to gain employment in the cities. The new workers exchange labor for wages in a wide variety of work sectors. According to China's National Bureau of Statistics data from March 25, 2009, by the end of 2008, China's migrant workers totaled 225 million, of which approximately 140 million are employed outside their native townships. According to *The Research Report on China's Migrant Workers* by the State Council Research Office in April 2006, the number of migrant workers has grown to surpass the number of traditional workers and has become the main force of China's contemporary working class. For instance, official data showed that there are about 4 million migrants in Beijing, which account for 30% of the municipality's total population.

Chinese migrant workers' contribution to the world comes at the cost of low wages and limited access to social welfare services. According to *The Survey on the Quality of Migrant Workers' Life* by the National Bureau of Statistics in October 2006, the average monthly income of a migrant worker is 966 Yuan (about 100 euros). According to the data released by the Ministry of Human Resources and Social Security in September 2009, the average monthly wage for migrant workers was around 1400 Yuan (about 150 euro). In 2009, Beijing Migrant Workers' Home conducted a small sample survey showing that, in Suzhou, workers salaries dropped from 1,987 Yuan (about 215 euros) to 1,402 Yuan (about 150 euros) due to the economic crisis; in Shenzhen, workers salaries dropped from 1,476 Yuan (about 160 euros) to 1,258 Yuan (about 135 euros) due to the economic crisis.

The National Bureau of Statistics reported in October 2006 that male migrant workers accounted for 65% of the sampled population, female accounted for 35%. Shenzhen Municipal Bureau of Personnel reported in 2006 that male migrant workers accounted for 48%, female accounted for 52% in enterprises in Shenzhen.

2 Überblick

2.1 Wer sind die neuen Arbeiter?

Als „neue Arbeiter" werden jene Frauen und Männer bezeichnet, die zwar als Bauern registriert sind, ihr Heimatdorf und die landwirtschaftliche Produktion jedoch verlassen haben, um in der Stadt eine Anstellung zu finden. Die neuen Arbeiter sind in vielen verschiedenen Berufsfeldern vertreten. Man geht davon aus, dass die Zahl der chinesischen Wanderarbeiter im Jahr 2008 etwa 140 Millionen betrug (Nationales Amt für Statistik, 2009). Dieser Begriff umfasst jene Personen, die außerhalb ihrer Heimatgemeinde arbeiten. Die Zahl der Wanderarbeiter übersteigt mittlerweile die der ortsansässigen Arbeiter. Somit sind Wanderarbeiter zur wichtigsten Arbeitskraft im heutigen China geworden (*Forschungsbericht über die Wanderarbeit in China,* Forschungsbüro des Staatsrates, 2006). Offizielle Daten belegen, dass in Peking ungefähr vier Millionen Wanderarbeiter leben, sie machen 30% der Bevölkerung in der chinesischen Großstadt.

Für den Beitrag der Wanderarbeiter zum chinesischen Wirtschaftboom erhalten diese im Gegenzug extrem niedrige Löhne und einen stark eingeschränkten Zugang zu Sozialleistungen. Das durchschnittliche Monatseinkommen eines Wanderarbeiters lag im Jahr 2006 bei 966 Yuan, was ungefähr dem Wert von 100 Euro entspricht (*Umfrage zur Lebensqualität von Wanderarbeitern,* Nationales Amt für Statistik, 2006). Im Jahr 2009 lag der monatliche Durchschnittslohn für Wanderarbeiter bei 1400 Yuan, ca. 150 Euro (Chinesisches Ministerium für Arbeit und Soziales). 2009 führte die gemeinnützige Organisation Migrant Workers' Home in Peking eine repräsentative Umfrage durch, nach der die Löhne von Arbeitern durch die Wirtschaftskrise in Suzhou von durchschnittlich 1.987 Yuan auf 1.402 Yuan und in Shenzhen von 1.476 Yuan auf 1.258 Yuan sanken.

Eine 2006 durchgeführte Erhebung des Nationalen Amtes für Statistik ergab ein Geschlechterverhältnis von 65% Männern und 35% Frauen unter den Wanderarbeitern. Das städtische Personalamt in Shenzhen meldete 2006 ein Verhältnis von 48% Männern und 52% Frauen in den Unternehmen im Stadtgebiet von Shenzen.

2.2 打工第一代和打工新生代 的对比

对打工群体的划分		出生年代	经历	认同
第一代打工者		70年代及之前出生	当过农民，会种地。80年代开始出来打工，很多是季节性工人。	认为农村是自己的归宿，认为最后要回到农村度过晚年
新生代打工者（占整个打工者群体人数的60%）	第二代打工者	80年代出生的	很多没有当过真正的农民，大多长年在外地打工	虽然没有当过农民，但是，因为觉得无法在城市购房和长期稳定的工作，所以处于迷茫之中
	第三代打工者	90年代出生的	大都没有种过地，很多在城市出生和长大	对土地和农村没有认同， 希望在城市落脚生根

2.2 Experiences and identity of the first and new generation of migrant workers

Categorizing		Time of Birth	Experiences	Identity
First generation		Born in the 1970s and before	They were farmers before.	They consider the homeland in the countryside as their destiny.
New generation (share more than 60% of the migrant workers' population)	Second generation	Born in the 1980s	They may have helped with cropping, but were never real farmers.	They are not sure whether they should fight for their rights in the cities or they should accept their fate returning to the countryside when they are old.
	Third generation	Born in the 1990s	Most of them never did any farming work, and many were born and grow up in cities.	They have no identity to farmland and the countryside. They think that they belong to the city.

2.2 Erfahrungen und Identität der ersten und der neuen Generation von Wanderarbeitern

Kategorisierung		Geburtsdatum	Erfahrungen	Identität
Erste Generation		Geboren in den 1970er Jahren oder früher	Sie sind ehemalige Bauern.	Sie fühlen sich mit ihrem Heimatdorf verbunden.
Neue Generation (mehr als 60% der Population der Wanderarbeiter)	Zweite Generation	Geboren in den 1980er Jahren	Sie haben möglicherweise bei der Ernte geholfen, waren aber nie als Bauern im eigentlichen Sinne tätig.	Sie sind unsicher, ob sie in den Städten für ihre Rechte kämpfen oder ihr Schicksal akzeptieren und im Alter in das Heimatdorf zurückkehren sollen.
	Dritte Generation	Geboren in den 1990er Jahren	Sie haben meist keine Erfahrungen in der Landwirtschaft und sind in der Stadt aufgewachsen.	Sie sind in ihrer Identität nicht mit der bäuerlicher Arbeit oder dem Landleben verbunden, sondern fühlen sich in der Stadt zu Hause.

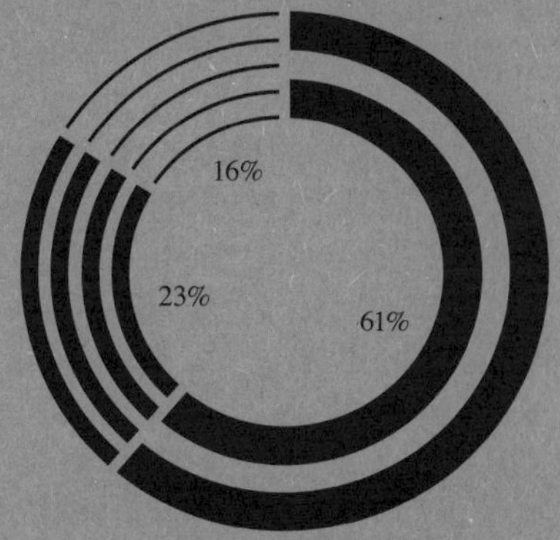

Age structure of migrant workers / Altersstruktur der Wanderarbeiter

61% 16–30岁 / 16–30 years old / 16–30 Jahre
23% 31–40岁 / 31–40 years old / 31–40 Jahre
16% 41岁以上 / above 41 years old / 41 Jahre oder älter

Source: *The Research Report on China's Migrant Workers* by the State Council Research Office, April 2006 / Quelle: *Der Forschungsbericht zu Chinas Wanderarbeitern* des Forschungsbüros des Staatsrates, April 2006

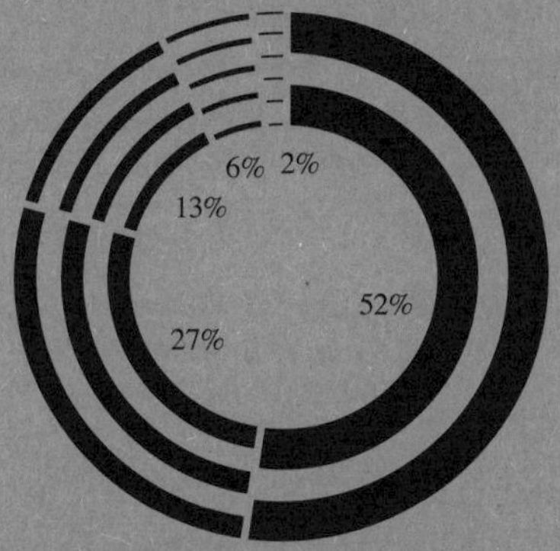

Education level of migrant workers / Bildungsgrad der Wanderarbeiter

2% 文盲和半文盲 / Illiterate and Semi-illiterate / Teilweise oder ganz Analphabeten
13% 小学 / Primary School / Grundschule
52% 初中 / Secondary School / Haupt- oder Realschule
27 % 高中 / High School / Gymnasium
6% 大学 / College and Higher / FH, Universität und Höher

Source: *The Survey on the Quality of Migrant Workers' Life* by the National Bureau of Statistics Survey Services Center's, October 2006 / Quelle: *Umfrage zur Lebensqualität von Wanderarbeitern* des Nationalen Amtes für Statistik, Oktober 2006

2.3 打工30年流动的历史图

1978年，改革开放。从1950年到1957年中国实行了土地改革，分田到户，农民成了小块土地的所有者和独立经营的个体劳动者。农民拥有了自己私有的土地。从1956年到1962年，中国实行了农业生产的集体化道路；土地实行了集体所有制。1978年，开始实行农村家庭联产承包责任制，是指农户以家庭为单位向集体承包土地等生产资料和生产任务的农村生产责任制形式。 具体说就是：交够国家的，留足集体的，剩下都是自己的。

1992年，邓小平南巡。1992年，邓小平南巡讲话，加快了改革开放与经济建设的步伐，跨地域外出打工的人数大幅度增加。 中国开始了以“经济建设为中心”的发展阶段，从此，一切为经济发展让路，逐步走上了今天中国经济快速发展，但是贫富差距巨大和社会矛盾突出的局面。

2003年，收容遣送制度取消，孙志刚事件。2003年3月17日，一位在广州打工的大学毕业生孙志刚因为没有办理暂住证被收容，并于20日死亡，尸检结果认为，孙志刚是遭毒打而导致死亡的。这个事件在全国引起巨大反响。许志永等几位律师联合上书全国人大，推动立法改革， 收容遣送制度取消，打工者身心获得解放。

2008年，《劳动合同法》实施，金融危机。2008年，《劳动合同法》实施，协调新时期劳资关系，维护打工者权益。2009年金融危机冲击中国。中国国家统计局在2009年3月25日发布的数据称，中国春节后外出移民工的失业率达到了17%左右的水平，约有2300～2500万外出移民工失业。2009年9月15日国家统计局公布，截至6月底， 移民工中已就业的逾97%。国家统计局2010年1月21日公布，中国在2009年仍然保持了国内生产总值为比上年增长8.7%的经济发展速度。

2.3 Mapping of the thirty year history of migration

1978, Reform and opening-up: From 1950 to 1957, China implemented a land reform, dividing up land and distributing it to each household, farmers became small landowners and independent workers on their own private land. From 1956 to 1962, China implemented an agricultural collectivization.

In 1978, the introduction of *the rural household contract system:* Each household made a contract with the collective/ its village committee and became a unit of production. China's economy started opening up to the outside world.

1992, Deng Xiaoping's southern tour: In 1992, Deng Xiaoping's southern tour speech, which called for accelerating the pace of reform and opening up, resulted in increasing rural-urban migration. China began to place economic growth at the center of its development, which eventually led to a economic miracle and an increasingly large gap between the rich and the poor. China is now witnessing huge social conflicts.

2003, *The detention and repatriation regulation* was abolished: On March 17, 2003, a university graduate, Sun Zhigang, was detained in Guangzhou because he did not have a temporary residence permit. He died three days later. Autopsy revealed that Sun had been beaten to death. This case caused uproar across the nation. Xu Zhiyong and several other lawyers sent a joint letter to the National People's Congress to promote legislative reform. As a result, the detention and repatriation system was abolished, which signaled a step towards migrant workers' physical and mental liberation.

2008, The implementation of the *Labor Contract law:* The financial crisis hit. In 2008, the *Labor contract law* was implemented, introducing a new era of labor relations and the safeguarding of the rights and interests of migrant workers. In 2009, the financial crisis hit, and China's National Bureau of Statistics (March 2009) released data showing that the unemployment rate among Chinese migrant workers reached around 17%, about 23 ~ 25 million. The National Bureau of Statistics survey (September 2009) showed that, at the end of June, more than 97% migrant workers had been employed. National Bureau of Statistics (January 2010) announced that China in 2009 maintained an economic growth rate of 8.7% over the previous year despite of the financial crisis.

2.3 Dreißig Jahre Migration im Überblick

1978, Reform und Öffnung: Von 1950 bis 1957 setzte die chinesische Regierung eine Bodenreform um. Durch die Verteilung von landwirtschaftlicher Fläche an die Haushalte wurden mittellose Bauern zu Kleingrundbesitzern, die selbstständig ihren eigenen Grund und Boden bewirtschaften konnten. Bauern besaßen nun ein privates Grundeigentum. In den Jahren von 1956 bis 1962 betrieb die Regierung die Kollektivierung der Landwirtschaft. Im Jahr 1978 beschloss das dritte Plenum des 11. Parteitages die Einführung eines *Vertragssystems für ländliche Haushalte*. Dem System folgend mussten alle Haushalte Verträge mit ihren Genossenschaften bzw. mit ihren Dorfkomitees abschließen, um so den Status der eigenständigen Produktionseinheit zu erhalten. Chinas Wirtschaft begann sich der Außenwelt zu öffnen.

1992, Deng Xiaopings Reise in den Süden: Nach Deng Xiaopings Rede anlässlich seiner Reise in den Süden im Jahr 1992, in der er die Beschleunigung der Reformen und der Öffnung forderte, nahm die Abwanderung vom Land in die Städte zu. Die chinesische Regierung begann, wirtschaftliches Wachstum in den Mittelpunkt der Entwicklung Chinas zu stellen. Diese Politik führte schließlich zum chinesischen Wirtschaftswunder und im gleichen Zug zu einer immer größer werdenden Kluft zwischen Arm und Reich.

2003, Das System *Verhaftung und Rückführung* wurde abgeschafft: Am 17. März 2003 wurde der Student Sun Zhigang in Guangzhou verhaftet, da er keine Aufenthaltsgenehmigung besaß. Er starb drei Tage später. Die Autopsie offenbarte, dass Sun tot geprügelt worden war. Sein Fall erregte landesweites Aufsehen. Der Rechtswissenschaftler Xu Zhiyong und weitere Anwälte verfassten einen gemeinsamen Brief an den nationalen Volkskongress mit der Forderung nach gesetzlichen Reformen. In der Folge wurde das System „Verhaftung und Rückführung" abgeschafft, womit ein Schritt hin zur äußeren und geistigen Befreiung der Wanderarbeiter getan war.

2008, Verabschiedung des *Arbeitsvertragsrechts:* 2008 trat das *Arbeitsvertragsrecht* in Kraft und leitete eine neue Ära der Arbeitsbeziehungen und des Schutzes der Rechte und Interessen von Wanderarbeitern ein. Im Jahr 2009 machten sich die Auswirkungen der Finanzkrise bemerkbar. Die Arbeitslosenquote unter chinesischen Wanderabeitern betrug zu dem Zeitpunkt 17% (Nationales Amt für Statistik in China, 2009). Noch im Juni 2009 hatten über 97% der Wanderarbeiter einen Arbeitsplatz (Nationales Amt für Statistik, September 2009). Das chinesische Wirtschaftswachstum betrug 2009 noch immer 8,7% (Nationales Amt für Statistik, Januar 2010).

3 工人权益

3.1 工资拖欠

据新华社2004年8月26日公布的数字显示，截至2004年8月6日，全国共拖欠移民工工资是32400 亿元，但同期已解决拖欠移民工工资28300 亿元，占拖欠总额的87%； 根据国家统计局服务业调查中心于2006年10月公布的“农民工生活质量调查”显示，在所调查的移民工中，被拖欠过报酬的有5741人，占被调查总数的20%，其中经常被拖欠的占被拖欠过报酬移民工的14%，偶尔被拖欠的占86%。移民工被拖欠报酬时间最短的有1 个月，最长的达到8年，平均是被拖欠了4个月。

国务院研究室2006年发布《中国农民工调研报告》显示，移民工工资领取方式主要有两种：一种方式是按月领取，为60%；另一种方式是按年领取，为28%。在被调查者中，基本能按时领取工资的达到48%，有时延期和经常延期的比例达到36%和16%。

为了摸清移民工底数及外出返乡情况，国家统计局利用移民工返乡过节的时机，于2009年初在全国31个省、857个县、7100个村和68000个农村住户开展了一次大规模的抽样调查。国家统计局2009年3月25日发布调查报告显示，6%的返乡移民工被拖欠工资。对于受金融危机影响而返回的移民工，因企业关停而返乡的移民工中有13%被拖欠了工资；因企业裁员而返乡的移民工中有6%被拖欠了工资。

3 Workers’ rights

3.1 Wage arrears

According to the Xinhua News Agency (August 2004), the country owed 32.4 billion yuan in wages to migrant workers. 28.3 billion were settled before the news release, accounting for 87% of the debt. *The Survey on the Quality of Migrant Workers’ Life* (National Bureau of Statistics, October 2006) revealed that 20% of the sampled population had been owed wages. 14% of them have had encountered this problem frequently; 86% have encountered this problem occasionally. The shortest time in which the wage was paid back was in 1 month and the longest was 8 years, the average arrear time was 4 months.

60% of the workers are paid on a monthly basis, whereas 28% are paid annually (State Council Research Office, 2006). According to the same survey, 48% receive their wages on time; 16% are often not paid on time and 36% sometimes experienced delayed payments. The National Bureau of Statistics conducted a survey during Chinese New Year when migrants rushed home for the holidays in 2009. The survey covered 31 provinces and 68,000 rural households. The results show that 6% of the migrant workers had not received their wages in full. Of those who returned home due to the impact of the financial crisis, 13% were owed wages.

3 Arbeiterrechte

3.1 Lohnrückstände

Laut einer im August 2004 veröffentlichten Meldung der chinesischen Presseagentur Xinhua schuldete der Staat bis dato seinen Wanderarbeitern Löhne in Höhe von 32,4 Milliarden Yuan. Davon wurden 28,3 Milliarden Yuan und somit 87% der Gesamtschulden vor Veröffentlichung der Pressemeldung beglichen. Die *Umfrage zur Lebensqualität von Wanderarbeitern* (Nationales Amt für Statistik, Oktober 2006) ergab, dass 20% der Wanderarbeiter mindestens einmal ihren Lohn zu spät erhalten haben. Von ihnen sind 14% häufig betroffen; 86% begegnen diesem Problem gelegentlich. Die Dauer des Verzugs der Lohnnachzahlung liegt zwischen einem Monat und 8 Jahren, wobei die durchschnittliche Verzugszeit vier Monate beträgt. 60% der Wanderarbeiter erhalten ihren Lohn monatlich, während 28% jährlich vergütet werden (Forschungsbüro des Staatsrates, 2006). Derselben Umfrage zufolge erhalten 48% der Arbeiter ihren Lohn pünktlich. 16% sind häufig von Lohnrückständen betroffen, 36% begegnen dem Problem seltener. Das Nationale Amt für Statistik führte 2009 während des chinesischen Neujahrsfestes eine Umfrage unter den Wanderarbeitern durch, da viele von ihnen über die Feiertage in die ländliche Heimat fuhren. Die Umfrage erstreckte sich über 31 Provinzen und 68.000 Haushalte. Die Ergebnisse zeigen, dass 6% der Wanderarbeiter vor ihrer Heimkehr zum Neujahrsfest nicht ihren vollen Lohn erhalten haben. Bei jenen, die aufgrund der Finanzkrise ihren Arbeitsplatz verloren hatten, bestanden in 13% der Fälle Lohnrückstände.

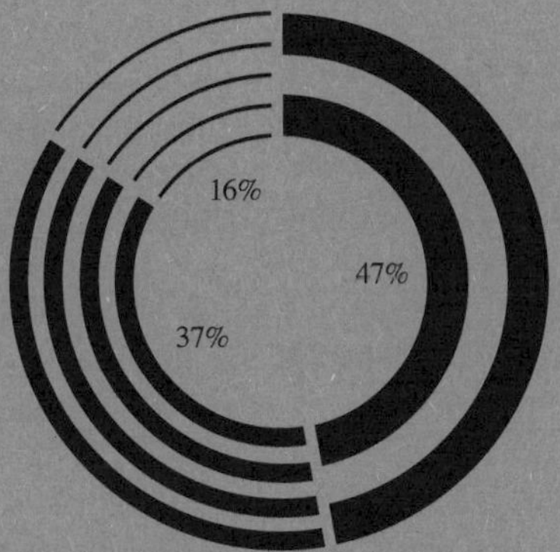

Weekly working time of migrant workers / Wochenarbeitszeit of migrant workers

47% 一周工作7天 / 7 Day Work Week / 7-Tage-Woche

37% 一周工作6天 / 6 Day Work Week / 6-Tage-Woche

16% 一周工作5天 / 5 Day Work Week / 5-Tage-Woche

The Survey on the Quality of Migrant Workers’ Life by the National Bureau of Statistics Survey Services Center’s, October 2006 / *Umfrage zur Lebensqualität von Wanderarbeitern* des Nationalen Amtes für Statistik, Oktober 2006

3.2 工作条件和工伤事故

人力资源和社会保障部公布，2008年认定的近一百万工伤人员中，百分之八十以上是移民工；中国每年工伤事故死亡近二万人，工伤造成的永久性伤残人数超过十万人。中国社会科学院经济研究所2008年11月3日发布的《农村迁移工人的劳动保护问题》研究报告称，当前，移民工劳动保护十分薄弱，54%的被调查者处在不良工作环境中，他们的工作环境至少符合"有毒"、"粉尘"、"噪音"、"潮湿"和"高空"5个选项中的一项。

国家统计局2009年9月15日公布调查数据显示，截至6月底，全国农村跨地域外出务工劳动力15097万人。其中参加养老保险人数为2380万人(16%)，参加医疗保险人数为4153万人(28%)，参加失业保险人数为1518万人(10%)，参加工伤保险人数为5054万人(34%)。

根据国家统计局服务业调查中心在2006年10月所做的"农民工生活质量调查"显示，移民工平均每周工作6.3天，其中，47%每周工作7天，37%每周工作6天，16%每周工作时间为5天。移民工平均每天工作9小时，其中，每天工作8小时的占53。每天工作9-10小时的占26%，每天工作11至12小时的占11%，有3%平均每天工作时间在12小时以上。

根据工友之家的案例调查发现，很多在农贸市场摆摊和自家经营小生意的打工者，每天工作时间达到15个小时左右，而且从来没有休息日。移民工平均每天工作9小时，其中，每天工作8小时的占53。每天工作9至10小时的占26%，每天工作11至12小时的占11%，有3%平均每天工作时间在12小时以上。根据工友之家的案例调查发现，很多在农贸市场摆摊和自家经营小生意的打工者，每天工作时间达到15个小时左右，而且从来没有休息日。

3.2 Working conditions and workplace injuries

80% of the nearly one million workers who had work-related injuries were migrant workers (Ministry of Human Resources and Social Security in China, 2008). Nearly 20,000 people are killed each year in China due to work related accidents and more than 100,000 people are permanently disabled due to work-related injuries. The Institute of Economics at the Chinese Academy of Social Sciences released a report titled *Rural Migrant Workers and Labor Protection Issues* in November 2008, which indicated that 54% of the respondents work in poor working environments and are thus exposed to either toxicity, dust, noise, dampness or high altitude. But only 34% have work injury insurance. In addition, only 16% have pension insurance, 28% have medical insurance, and only 10% have unemployment insurance (National Bureau of Statistics in China). Migrant workers work for 9 hours per day on average, of which 53% work for 8 hours per day; 26% work for 9–10 hours per day, and 11% work for 11–12 hours per day, and 3% work for 12 or more hours a day. Many migrant workers who run stalls in markets or who owned small businesses work an average of 15 hours a day, with no break throughout a year (Migrant Workers' Home).

3.2 Arbeitsbedingungen und -unfälle

Bei 80% der knapp einer Millionen Unfälle am Arbeitsplatz sind Wanderarbeiter betroffen (Ministerium für Arbeit und soziale Sicherheit in China, 2008). Jedes Jahr sterben knapp 20.000 Menschen infolge eines Arbeitsunfalls; mehr als 100.000 Arbeiter tragen bleibende Schäden davon. Das Wirtschaftsinstitut der chinesischen Akademie der Sozialwissenschaften veröffentlichte im November 2008 den Bericht *Ländliche Zuwanderung von Arbeitskräften und Fragen des Arbeitsschutzes*. Daraus ging hervor, dass 54% der Arbeiter in einem mangelhaften Arbeitsumfeld tätig sind und somit entweder Giftstoffen, Staub, Lärm, Feuchtigkeit oder großen Höhen ausgesetzt sind. Jedoch sind lediglich 34% im Falle eines Arbeitsunfalls versichert. Außerdem sind nur 16% der Wanderarbeiter rentenversichert, 28% sind krankenversichert und nur 10% haben eine Arbeitslosenversicherung (Nationales Amt für Statistik in China). Wanderarbeiter arbeiten durchschnittlich 9 Stunden pro Tag: 53% arbeiten 8 Stunden, 26% arbeiten 9 bis 10 Stunden, weitere 11% arbeiten 11 bis 12 Stunden und 3% arbeiten 12 Stunden und mehr pro Tag. Viele Wanderarbeiter, die Marktstände betreiben oder ähnliche Kleinbetriebe führen, arbeiten ohne Ruhetage einzulegen durchschnittlich 15 Stunden pro Tag (Migrant Workers' Home).

3.3 居住状况

很多打工者已经在城市打工10年甚至20年了，他们在城市工作和生活，为城市发展和经济建设做出了巨大的贡献，但是他们在城市居住状况却很差：打工者在城市仍然是暂住的身份；在居住条件上仍然处于及其简单和简陋的临时性居住状况；很多打工者家庭处于不团圆状况，多数是子女没有条件跟随父母居住，也有一些是夫妻分居两地；新生代打工者多数已经没有务农经验、没有耕地、没有对农民身份的认同、在城市工作和生活并对长期在城市生活充满渴望，但是，他们的理想和现实差距巨大。

根据国家统计局服务业调查中心在2006年10月所做的"农民工生活质量调查"显示：有29%的移民工居住在集体宿舍里；有20%的人居住在缺乏厨卫设施的房间里；8%的人居住在工作地点；6%的人居住在临时搭建的工棚里；还有13%的移民工在城里没有住所，只能往返于城乡之间。人民大学学生在2007年社会实践调查中发现，在北京的一个打工者聚居区十里河村，82%的移民工租住当地村民的私房，18%的移民工住在宿舍或工棚。根据北京工友之家2009年在北京皮村的调查显示，打工者在北京皮村平均每人的居住面积是4到5平米（2006年某调查数据显示，北京户籍人口居住面积20平方米），在深圳是3平米，在苏州是4平米。在2006年月10月公布的数据显示，农民工平均月收入966元，63%的进城务工人员每月的住房花费在200元左右，也就是很大一部分人月收入的20%以上用于租房子。中国的法律规定，移民工只能在户口所在地农村老家参加选举。在这种情况下，绝大多数移民工就被排除在政治生活之外，他们既不参加老家的选举（因为距离远而且已经脱离那里的生活）；也不参加城市社区和工作场所的选举（因为户口不在当地所以没有选举资格）。2008年3月，首次产生了三名移民工全国人大代表。

3.3 Residential status

Many migrant workers have been living and working in the city for ten to twenty years, contributing greatly to the urban development. This fact does not match the migrant workers' residential status. Facing very poor living conditions in the city, they are still considered temporary residents. Many migrant worker family members cannot live together. Younger generation migrants mostly do not know how to farm and do not identify themselves with peasants as they are accustomed to city lives, however there is a big gap between their identity and the reality. The figures confirm precarious living conditions.

According to *The Survey on the Quality of Migrant Workers' Life* (National Bureau of Statistics, 2006) 29% of the migrant workers lived in dormitories; 20% lived in housing with no kitchen and bathroom facilities; 8% lived at the workplace; 6% lived in temporary structures, and 13% had no shelter in the city so that they had to shuttle between the city and the countryside. A survey by some students from People's University in 2007 found out that 82% of the migrant workers in Shilihe Village near Beijing rented from local villagers while 18% lived in dormitories or temporary structures provided by their employers. The average living area of migrants in Picun Village in Beijing was 4 to 5 square meters (Migrant Workers' Home, 2009) whereas the living area of Beijing residents was 20 square meters per capita (survey data, 2006); in Shenzhen, living area was 3 square meters, and 4 square meters in Suzhou. Migrant workers spend approximately 20% of their monthly income on rent. According to the Chinese law, migrant workers are only eligible to participate in the election at the place of their household registration in their hometown. In this way, they are excluded from the political participation in cities where they work and live. In March 2008, three migrant workers became National People's Congress representatives for the first time in Chinese history.

3.3 Aufenthaltsstatus

Viele Wanderarbeiter leben und arbeiten seit 10 bis 20 Jahren in der Stadt und tragen in hohem Maße zur urbanen Entwicklung bei. Dieser Tatsache steht der Aufenthaltsstatus der Wanderarbeiter gegenüber. Sie leben in der Stadt unter äußerst ärmlichen Bedingungen und werden immer noch als Einwohner auf Zeit angesehen. Viele Wanderarbeiterfamilien können nicht zusammenleben. Die neue Generation verfügt größtenteils über keinerlei Erfahrung in der Landwirtschaft. Sie identifizieren sich nicht mit dem bäuerlichen Leben, da sie in der Stadt aufgewachsen sind. Zwischen ihrem Identitätsgefühl und den realen Bedingungen besteht eine große Diskrepanz.

Die prekäre Wohnsituation der Wanderarbeiter wird durch die *Umfrage zur Lebensqualität von Wanderarbeitern* (Nationales Amt für Statistik, 2006) bestätigt: 29% der Wanderarbeiter leben in Wohnheimen; 20% leben in Unterkünften ohne Küche und Bad; 8% wohnen am Arbeitsplatz, 6% in provisorischen Unterkünften und 13% verfügen über keine Unterkunft in der Stadt, sondern pendeln zwischen dem Arbeitsplatz und dem Wohnort auf dem Land. Eine von Studenten der Volksuniversität Peking im Jahr 2007 durchgeführte Untersuchung ergab, dass 82% der Wanderarbeiter im Dorf Shilihe bei Peking bei der Dorfbevölkerung zur Miete wohnen, während 18% in Wohnheimen oder provisorischen Unterkünften leben, die ihnen vom Arbeitgeber zur Verfügung gestellt werden. Die durchschnittliche Wohnfläche eines Wanderarbeiters im Dorf Picun beläuft sich auf 4 bis 5 qm (Migrant Workers' Home, 2009), während die durchschnittliche Wohnfläche pro Einwohner in Peking nach einer Umfrage von 2006 20 qm beträgt. Dieselbe Umfrage ergab, dass in Shenzhen die Wohnfläche eines Wanderarbeiters 3 qm und in Suzhou 4 qm beträgt. Für die Miete dieses Wohnraumes wenden Wanderarbeiter durchschnittlich 20% ihrer Monatseinkünfte auf. Außerdem sind Wanderarbeiter zwar in ihrem Geburtsort nach chinesischem Recht wahlberechtigt, in den Städten, in denen diese Menschen leben und arbeiten, sind sie jedoch von der politischen Teilhabe ausgeschlossen. Im März 2008 wurden erstmals in der Geschichte Chinas drei Wanderarbeiter als Abgeordnete in den nationalen Volkskongress gewählt.

3.4 北京和深圳打工者家庭的家庭团圆状况 / Family life of migrant workers / Vergleich familiärer Lebensverhältnisse der Wanderarbeiter

北京和深圳打工者家庭的家庭团圆状况 / Family life of migrant workers / Die familiären Lebensverhältnisse der Wanderarbeiter	北京皮村 / Picun Village / Dorf Picun	深圳某工厂/ A factory in Shenzhen / Eine Fabrik in Shenzhen
全家团圆(夫妻和所有孩子都在一起) / All family members live together / Die ganze Familie lebt zusammen	71%	20%
夫妻团圆 / Husbands and wives are together / Eheleute leben zusammen	98%	86%
被留在老家的孩子的比例 / Left-behind Children in the countryside / Zurückgelassene Kinder auf dem Land	36%	74%

(资料来源:北京工友之家的打工者居住现状和未来发展调查报告, 2009年 / *Report on Migrant Workers Residential Status and Future Perspectives,* by Beijing Migrant Workers' Home in 2009 / *Bericht über die Wohnsituation von Wanderarbeitern und ihre Zukunftsperspektiven* von Migrant Workers' Home, Peking 2009)

4 制度变迁

4.1 居住权

1958年，以《中华人民共和国户口登记条例》为标志，中国政府开始对人口自由流动实行严格限制，明确将城乡居民区分为"农业户口"和"非农业户口"两种不同户籍。"二元制"户籍管理模式，使非农人口较农业人口得到了国家给予的更多优惠和利益保障；农民没有劳保、医保、住房等事关生计的种种保障。最突出的就是在就业和受教育两方面，如有的城市规定：某些行业和工种必须持有所在城市的户口才能被录用。教育方面也是如此，许多持农业户口者在城市里工作多年，有稳定收入，但因为子女没有所在城市的户口，不得不交纳一定的借读费，平等受教育的权利由于"户籍制度"而失去。

1982年的《城市流浪乞讨人员收容遣送办法》从政策上是对无生活来源的人的救助，而在实际的执行中，成为了随意收容遣送进城务工人员的恶法。1985年，公安部颁布了《关于城镇暂住人口管理的若干规定》，决定对流动人口实行"暂住证"制度，允许流动人口在城市暂时居住。

2003年8月，实施《城市生活无着落人员救助管理办法，1982年5月国务院发布的《城市流浪乞讨人员收容遣送办法》同时废止。从2004年开始，沈阳市，成都市，昆明市，浙江省先后开始试行和实行针对移民工的"居住证"制度，希望逐步让在城市稳定居住和生活的移民群体享受和当地人口一样的待遇。2010年，广东省开始实行居住证制度，北京也计划实行居住证制度.

养老保险：《城镇企业职工基本养老保险关系转移接续暂行办法》规定，从2010年1月1日起施行。包括移民工在内的参加城镇企业职工基本养老保险的人员，其基本养老保险可在跨省就业时随同转移；

医疗保障：《流动就业人员基本医疗保障关系转接接续暂行办法》规定，从2010年7月1日开始，流动人员跨省就业时可以转移自己的医保关系，移民工可在就业地参加当地的职工基本医疗保险，回农村后可带回，转为新型农村合作医疗保险，而且不会中断。

保护劳动权力的相关法律：劳动合同法《劳动合同法》自2008年1月1日起施行，协调新时期劳资关系，维护移民工权益。就业促进法《就业促进法》自2008年1月1日起施行，移民工进城就业享有与城镇劳动者平等的劳动权利，不得在移民工进城就业上设置歧视性限制。

4 Policy Evolution

4.1 Residential Rights

In 1958, the Chinese government adopted *Household Registration Regulations of the People's Republic of China.* It was the starting point of the strict control of population movements that divided the Chinese into "urban residents" and "rural residents". The rural population is not entitled to social security, medical, housing and other kinds of safeguards concerning livelihoods. The most prominent inequality is in both employment and education. Some city administrations regulate that only urban residents can be hired in certain industries or trades. Children of migrants have no equal access to education in the cities.

In 1982, *The Detention and Repatriation Regulations of the Homeless and Beggars* was issued. The policy itself addressed how to assist people, but in the actual implementation, it was turned into a brutal tool to control the life of migrant workers. In 1985, the Ministry of Public Security promulgated the *Administration of Temporary Residents in the Urban Areas* and started to implement the *temporary residence permit* system to allow migrants to live in urban areas temporarily.

In August 2003, *The Administration and Assistance Measures for the Homeless and the Beggars* went into effect, the 1982 *The Detention and Repatriation Regulations of the Homeless and Beggars* was abolished simultaneously.

Beginning in 2004, Shenyang, Chengdu, Kunming and Zhejiang provinces started trials of implementing a *residence permit* system, hoping to assist the migrants to gradually make a stable life in the cities and to give migrant workers equal treatment as the local residents. Guangdong province introduced these residence permits in 2010. Beijing also plans to implement the system.

The trend in the social security system is positive because the *Provisional Procedure for the Transfer and Continuation of Urban Enterprise Workers' Pension Package* came into effect on January 1, 2010. The package stipulates that workers, including migrant workers, can transfer their pension package across regions around the country. Furthermore *The Provisional Procedure for Transfer and Continuation of Migrant Workers' Basic Medical Security Package* came into effect on July 1, 2010. Migrant workers are now able to transfer their medical security package without interruption to wherever they move, even back to the countryside, and the new rural cooperative medical insurance.

In addition, two new laws came into effect on January 1, 2008. One of these laws is *The Labor Contract Law* which safeguards the rights and interests of migrant workers, which started a new era of labor relations in China. Another is *The Employment Promotion Law,* which stipulates that migrant workers should enjoy equal working rights in cities, and no discriminatory restrictions should be imposed on the employment of migrant workers.

4 Die politische Entwicklung

4.1 Aufenthaltsrechte

1958 verabschiedet die chinesische Regierung das *Gesetz zur Haushaltsanmeldung*. Dies erlaubt eine bessere Kontrolle der chinesischen Binnenwanderung und hat gleichzeitig eine Teilung des chinesischen Volkes in Stadt- und Landbevölkerung zur Folge.

Im Gegensatz zur städtischen Bevölkerung bleibt der Landbevölkerung die Teilhabe am Sozialsystem mit seiner medizinischen Versorgung und der Absicherung des Lebensunterhalts verwehrt. Die augenfälligste Ungleichheit besteht in den Bereichen Arbeit und Bildung. In einigen Kommunen werden in bestimmten Industrie- und Gewerbezweigen nur registrierte Bewohner dieser Kommune beschäftigt. Kinder von Wanderarbeitern haben außerdem in den Städten nur eingeschränkten Zugang zu Bildungseinrichtungen.

1982 tritt das Gesetz zur *Verhaftung und Rückführung von Obdachlosen und Bettlern* in Kraft. Das ursprüngliche Ziel dieses Gesetzes war es, diese Menschen zu unterstützen. In der Praxis wird dieses Gesetz jedoch als brutales Werkzeug zur Kontrolle der Wanderarbeiter missbraucht.

Im Jahr 1985 verkündet das Ministerium für Öffentliche Sicherheit die *Gesetze für befristete Aufenthalte in städtischen Gebieten*. Diese Gesetzesänderung erlaubt den Wanderarbeitern einen befristeten Aufenthalt in der Stadt.

2003 tritt das Gesetz *Administrative Hilfsmaßnahmen für Obdachlose und Bettler* in Kraft, womit das Gesetz zur *Verhaftung und Rückführung von Obdachlosen und Bettlern* aus dem Jahr 1982 aufgehoben ist.

Im Jahr 2004 wird in den Provinzen Shenyang, Chengdu, Kunming und Zhejiang ein System für Aufenthaltsgenehmigungen auf Probe eingeführt. So hoffte man, Wanderarbeitern den allmählichen Übergang zu einem geordneten Leben in den Städten zu erleichtern und ihre Gleichberechtigung mit der städtischen Bevölkerung sicherzustellen. Dieses System für Aufenthaltsgenehmigungen wird 2010 auch in der Provinz Guangdong eingeführt. In Peking wird die Einführung noch geplant.

Eine positive Entwicklung ist auch bei den Sozialversicherungen zu erkennen. Das *Vorläufige Verfahren zur Umbuchung und Fortführung des Rentenpakets für Arbeitnehmer in städtischen Unternehmen* tritt zum 1. Januar 2010 in Kraft. Die Einführung dieses Verfahrens erlaubt es allen Arbeitnehmern die Renteneinzahlungen über Regionsgrenzen hinaus und somit landesweit zu transferieren. Zum 1. Juli desselben Jahres wurde ebenfalls das *Vorläufige Verfahren zur Umbuchung und Fortführung des Pakets für medizinische Grundversorgung für Wanderarbeiter* eingeführt. Dieses Gesetz erlaubt Wanderarbeitern, ihre Krankenversicherung bei einem Umzug mitzunehmen, ein Recht, das auch bei einer Rückkehr in das Heimatdorf Gültigkeit behält. Das medizinische Versorgungspaket kann direkt in eine neue Krankenversicherung für landwirtschaftliche Genossenschaften überführt werden.

Außerdem tritt bereits zum 1. Januar 2008 das *Arbeitsvertragsrecht* in Kraft, das Rechte und Interessen von Wanderarbeitern gegenüber Unternehmen stärkt. Für die Arbeitsverhältnisse in China beginnt damit eine neue Ära. Das ebenfalls zum Jahreswechsel 2007/2008 verabschiedete *Beschäftigungsförderungsgesetz* legt darüber hinaus fest, dass Wanderarbeiter in den Städten gleichberechtigt arbeiten und somit ihre Anstellung keinen diskriminierenden Beschränkungen unterliegen darf.

5　女工权益

《女职工劳动保护规定》明确规定，不得在女职工怀孕期、产期、哺乳期降低其基本工资，或者解除劳动合同。2008年一项由北京市和部分省区市的农民工法律援助工作站共同开展的调查显示，72%的人表示不知道这些规定，68%的人表示没有受到任何特殊保护。
根据国家统计局服务业调查中心在2006年10月所做的“农民工生活质量调查”显示，妇女可以带薪休产假的占被调查的女打工者的比重为20%。
在雇主家庭工作的家政工不受劳动法保护。法律专家指出，家政工与雇主之间的关系只属于“民事关系”。据不完全统计，中国有2千万名从事家政服务的打工者，其中很多家政工长期居住在雇主家里。据北京大学法学院妇女法律研究与服务中心和联合国妇女发展基金于2008年撰写的《关于家政工劳动权益保护的调研报告》显示，多数家政工要超时工作，且没有节假日。
西南政法大学外国家庭法及妇女理论研究中心在2009年11月所做的《我国农村妇女外出务工权益及其法律保障调查实证研究》（有效问卷2106份）发现，在受访者中，“不能与男性工作者同工同酬”的为19%。中国社会科学院妇女/性别研究中心对2398名打工者进行了调查，并于2008年公布《农村迁移工人在城市劳动力市场表现方面的性别差异》课题报告。报告显示，女性打工者平均月工资为910元，男性打工者为1100元，二者相差近200元。　与受教育程度相比，性别歧视是导致工资差异更主要的原因。课题组发现，工资差异中37%来源于教育程度等人力资本差别，而其余63%则是因为性别歧视。
湖南省社科院新农村建设研究中心于2006年的调查显示，在长沙务工的打工妹65%都走进了服务行业(这里指美容美发、保健按摩、休闲娱乐、酒店、餐馆等)，达5万余人，她们平均年龄为21岁。她们中82%未婚。调查对象当中，有48%在工作场所遭到挑逗或骚扰。在打工者聚居区，妇女从事着各种工作，如：卖菜，开小店，家政服务，在工厂上班等，也有部分妇女因为孩子小而主要在家里照顾孩子。在各大城市的居民区住着很多中产阶级家庭，为了服务于小区和这些家庭的生活，很多打工者在这里打工，从事的工作包括：保安，保洁，餐厅服务和家政服务等工作。

5　Rights and interests of women migrant workers

The *Female workers labor protection provision* clearly indicates that it is not allowed to lower women's wage or to dismiss labor contracts during the period of women's pregnancy, birth, breast-feeding. A survey done by the Migrant Workers' Legal Aid Stations in 2008 showed that 72% of the interviewees did not know these provisions; 68% did not receive any protection. According to *The Survey on the Quality of Migrant Workers' Life* by the National Bureau of Statistics in October 2006, only 20% women migrant workers enjoyed paid maternity leave.
A survey on *The work rights and legal protection of migrant women,* conducted by the Research Center of Foreign Family Law and Women's Studies at Southwest University of Political Science in 2009 showed that 19% of the interviewees did not enjoy equal pay for the same work due to sexual discrimination. A survey on *The gender difference of migrant workers in urban labor market performance,* by the Women's / Gender Studies Center of Chinese Academy of Social Sciences, was released in 2008. About 2400 migrant workers were interviewed. The report showed that the average monthly wage of female migrant workers was 910 yuan, while that of male was 1100 yuan. Compared with the level of education, gender discrimination is a major cause of this gap. According to the analysis, 37% of the wage gap is a result of different level of educational, and 63% is due to gender.
A survey done by the Center of Building New Countryside of Hunan Academy of Social Sciences in 2006 showed that, of the 50 thousand migrant women who worked in Changsha, 65% worked in the service sector. Their average age was 21 years. 82% of them were unmarried. 48% of the interviewees reported being sexually harassed at their workplaces.
China's big cities are filled up with middle-class residential compounds, where many migrant workers live and work. The life of middle-class people is supported by migrant workers who provide services including: guards, cleaning, restaurants, domestic work, etc. It is estimated that there are 20 million domestic workers in China, many of them live under the same roof with their masters. According to *The Report on Labor Rights of Domestic Workers* by Beijing University in 2008, most domestic workers worked overtime and enjoyed no breaks during holidays and weekends. The Chinese *Labor Contract Law* does not protect domestic workers.

5　Rechte und Interessen von Wanderarbeiterinnen

Die *Bestimmungen zum Schutz von Arbeiterinnen* verbieten unmissverständlich, Frauen während der Schwangerschaft, der Geburt oder der Stillzeit den Lohn zu kürzen oder ihre Arbeitsverträge aufzulösen. Eine von den juristischen Beratungsstellen für Wanderarbeiter durchgeführte Umfrage aus dem Jahr 2008 ergab, dass 72% der Befragten diese Regelungen nicht kennen und 68% der Frauen keinerlei Mutterschutz gewährt wird. Laut der *Umfrage zur Lebensqualität von Wanderarbeitern* des Nationalen Amtes für Statistik erhalten nur 20% der Wanderarbeiterinnen bezahlten Mutterschaftsurlaub.
Eine vom Forschungszentrum für internationales Familienrecht und Frauenstudien im Jahr 2009 an der Süd-West-Universität für Politologie durchgeführte Umfrage zu Arbeitnehmerrechten und rechtlichem Schutz von Wanderarbeiterinnen zeigt, dass 19% der befragten Frauen aufgrund sexueller Diskriminierung einen geringeren Lohn als Männer für die gleiche Arbeit erhalten. Im Jahr 2008 wurde die Untersuchung *Unterschiedliche Behandlung von Wanderarbeitern und Wanderarbeiterinnen auf dem städtischen Arbeitsmarkt* vom Zentrum für Frauen-/Genderstudien an der chinesischen Akademie der Sozialwissenschaften veröffentlicht. Die Untersuchung, für die 2.400 Wanderarbeiter befragt wurden, zeigt, dass das durchschnittliche Monatseinkommen von Wanderarbeiterinnen bei 910 Yuan liegt, während das Einkommen ihrer männlichen Kollegen 1.100 Yuan betrug. Der Hauptgrund für den Einkommensunterschied von 200 Yuan resultiert nicht in erster Linie aus dem geringeren Bildungsstand der Frauen (37%), sondern zu 63% aus einer Geschlechterdiskriminierung.
Eine Umfrage des Zentrums zur Förderung des ländlichen Raumes der Akademie der Sozialwissenschaften in Hunan aus dem Jahr 2006 belegt, dass 65% der insgesamt 50.000 Wanderarbeiterinnen in Changsha im Dienstleistungssektor tätig sind. Ihr durchschnittliches Alter beträgt 21 Jahre. Von diesen Frauen gaben 48% der Befragten an, am Arbeitsplatz sexueller Belästigung ausgesetzt zu sein.
In den Wanderarbeitergemeinschaften, die sich zum Teil in den Vororten der Großstädte oder in der Stadt befinden, gehen Frauen verschiedensten Arbeiten nach; sie leiten kleinere Supermärkte, arbeiten als Haushaltshilfe und Reinigungskraft oder in den Fabriken. In Chinas Großstädten gibt es sehr viele Wohnviertel für die Mittelschicht.

Viele Wanderarbeiter arbeiten in diesen Privathaushalten als Sicherheitskraft oder Reinigungshilfe. Nach Schätzungen sind in chinesischen Privathaushalten 20 Millionen Personen angestellt, wobei viele im Haus ihres Arbeitgebers wohnen. Laut eines Berichts zu Arbeitnehmerrechten von Hausangestellten, den die Universität Peking 2008 veröffentlicht hat, leisten die meisten Hausangestellten Überstunden und müssen auch an Feiertagen und Wochenenden arbeiten. Die *Arbeitsvertragsrechte* gelten für diese Hausangestellten in China nicht.

6 流动儿童

6.1 留守儿童

造成留守儿童的原因主要有以下几个方面:(1)户籍制度和地区分割的入学和升学制度。在原籍地入学可以免收学费。很多流动儿童随父母在打工地念到小学毕业后就回老家念初中和高中了,因为他们只能在原籍地考大学。(2)打工家庭收入低,因此没有经济条件把孩子带在身边;(3)打工者往往工作时间很长,没有时间照顾孩子; 。

由于流动儿童在城市很难进入公立学校,因此打工子弟学校应运而生。打工子弟学校是由私人开办的,长期以来不享受国家的教育投入,所以必须自负盈亏,而且多数打工子弟学校办学的首要目的是盈利,所以打工子弟学校在如何实现教书育人和经济受益目标上存在很大的挑战。打工子弟学校都建在打工者聚居区内。没有关于全国打工学校数量的统计。北京的打工子弟学校从90年代开始出现,到1998达到100多所,到了2008年估计到了近300所。到目前为止,在这300所中仅有63所获得北京市政府的批准。

关于城市流动儿童的规模和结构,目前还缺乏详细的测算。我们同样利用2005年全国1%人口抽样调查的抽样数据,据测算,当年中国城市0~17周岁流动儿童的数量为1212万,其中14周岁以下流动儿童900万。据估计,目前流动儿童的数量超过2000万。 打工子弟在生活和学习中面临很多困境。

在生活上,对比城市儿童他们家境贫寒,父母工作忙没有时间照顾他们,他们很多很早就开始承担家务和照顾弟妹;在学习上,由于父母工作的流动他们经常要转学,打工子弟学校学习条件也比较差。

6 The migrant children

6.1 The left-behind children

Many children are left behind in the countryside while the parents are working in the city, this is because: (1) The household registration system and the regional segmentation system for school administration and university entrance exams have interfered with children of migrant workers following their parents to migrate to urban life and schooling; (2) Since the income level of migrant families is much worse than that of urban families, it is hard for migrants to send their children to school in the cities; (3) The migrant workers tend to work long hours, so that they have no time to care for and raise their children.

As many migrant children have difficulties to be administrated in public schools, migrant workers have found schools for the children that moved to the city with their parents. All of them are private-run and work on a profit-oriented basis. Most of such schools get no official papers, so that they do not enjoy any state investment in education. There is no official statistics on the total number of schools for migrant children. The schools for migrant children in Beijing began to emerge from the early 90's, and the number reached more than 100 in 1998, and reached about 300 in 2008, out of which only 63 received official approval from the Beijing Municipal Government.

It is hard to estimate the total number of migrant children. According to the 2005 national census, there are about 12 million migrant children from aged 0 to 17 living across China, and about 9 million are under age of 14. However, it is estimated by unofficial sources that the total number of migrant children is more than 20 million.

6 Die Kinder der Wanderarbeiter

6.1 Die zurückgelassenen Kinder

Viele Kinder werden auf dem Land zurückgelassen, während ihre Eltern in den Städten arbeiten, (1) weil Gesetze, wie regionale Gliederungssysteme der Schulbehörden oder Aufnahmeprüfungen an Universitäten, den Zugang zu Bildung erschweren und somit der Nachzug der Kinder von Wanderarbeitern in die Stadt behindert wird; (2) weil die Einkommensverhältnisse der Wanderarbeiterfamilien bedeutend schlechter als jene der ortsansässigen Familien sind, sodass die Aufwendungen für städtische Schulen nur schwer zu leisten sind; (3) weil Wanderarbeiter in der Regel einen langen Arbeitstag haben und Zeit für Erziehung und Fürsorge kaum vorhanden ist.

Da viele Wanderarbeiterkinder Schwierigkeiten haben, an öffentlichen Schulen aufgenommen zu werden, wurden in den Städten speziell für die Kinder der Wanderarbeiter Schulen gegründet. Es handelt sich ausnahmslos um Privatschulen, die gewinnorientiert arbeiten. Die meisten dieser Schulen sind nicht offiziell anerkannt und sind somit auch von staatlichen Förderprogrammen ausgeschlossen. Es gibt keine offiziellen Statistiken über die Gesamtzahl dieser Schulen für Wanderarbeiterkinder. Die ersten Schulen eröffneten in Peking Anfang der Neunzigerjahre. 1998 erhöhte sich die Zahl auf über 100 und im Jahr 2008 wurden bereits etwa 300 dieser Schulen betrieben, von denen jedoch nur 63 von der Kommunalbehörde in Peking offiziell anerkannt waren.

Die Gesamtzahl der Wanderarbeiterkinder lässt sich nur schwer erfassen. Laut der Volkszählung von 2005 gibt es in ganz China etwa 12 Millionen Wanderarbeiterkinder zwischen 0 und 17 Jahren, von denen etwa 9 Millionen jünger als 14 Jahre sind. Inoffizielle Daten gehen allerdings von mehr als 20 Millionen Kindern aus.

6.2 北京流动儿童的数量和入学情况 （万）/ Migrant Workers and their children in Beijing (in 10 thousand) / Wanderarbeiter und ihre Kinder in Peking (in 10 Tsd.)

年份 / Year / Jahr	2000	2001	2003	2004	2005	2006	2007
北京外来人口数量 / Migrant population in Beijing / Wanderarbeiterbevölkerung in Peking	256	–*	308	–*	357	383	420
北京适龄流动儿童数量 (7到15岁) / School age migrant children in Beijing / Wanderarbeiterkinder im Schulalter in Peking	10	–*	24	29	38	37	41
北京市公办学校接收适龄流动儿童数量 / Migrant children in public schools in Beijing / Wanderarbeiterkinder an öffentlichen Schulen	–*	8	18	19	24	25	27
北京市公办学校接收适龄流动儿童数量占适龄儿童的比例 / The percentage of migrant children in public school / Anteil von Wanderarbeiterkindern an öffentlichen Schulen	–*	–*	75%	65%	64%	68%	66%

(资料来源:王芳, 北京市适龄流动儿童教育状况分析, www.sociology.cass.cn / Source of information: Wang Fang, *The schooling status of school age migrant children in Beijing*, www.sociology.cass.cn / Wang Fang, *Der Status von Wanderarbeiterkindern im Schulalter in Peking*, www.sociology.cass.cn)

* Data is unknown. / Daten sind nicht bekannt.

7　新工人文化

打工文化艺术博物馆

2008年，在香港乐施会的资助下，北京工友之家创办了打工文化艺术博物馆，博物馆中以文字和实物反应了改革开放三十年中移民工的历史。 2009年，新增展览内容“打工者居住状况”，以文字和图片反映了打工者在城市的居住条件，家庭团圆的状况，打工的稳定性，在老家的臆想居住状况，打工者聚居区的发展和打工者对未来发展的看法和打算。

新工人艺术团

“用歌声呐喊，以文艺维权”，新工人艺术团自2002年5月1日成立以来，坚持为移民工群体义务演出并开展权益宣传活动共计500余场次，现场观众超过10万人，已经出版发行了三张专辑唱片、两部戏剧、两部电影和多部纪录片。

新工人文化艺术节

北京工友之家在香港乐施会的资助下于2009年1月1日到3日主办了“第一届打工文化艺术节”，2009年10月24到28日举办了“第二届新工人文化艺术节”。 来自全国各地的劳工团体和打工者参加了文艺和戏剧演出、工作坊和各种其他活动。 这是新工人创造和展示自己文化的重要阵地，正如艺术节的口号所表达的：‘自己搭台，自己唱戏’。

打工子弟的绘画，摄影，游戏和儿童刊物

从2007年开始，北京工友之家在国际计划，儿童乐益会，摩根大通，南都基金会和希尔顿的资助下开展儿童绘画，摄影和游戏活动。我们通过这些活动丰富孩子们的生活并去真实反应和思考自己的生活，同时鼓励孩子们发出自己的声音。 儿童刊物《流动的心声》收录的都是孩子们的作品，每月印刷8000册，发到北京30多所打工子弟学校。

7　New Workers' Culture

The Culture and Art Museum of Migrant Workers: In 2008, with the support of Oxfam Hong Kong, The Migrant Workers' Home founded a museum dedicated to documenting the thirty years history of China's migrant workers. In 2009, the museum launched a new exhibition on *The residential status of migrant workers,* which portrays migrant workers' living conditions, the problem of family reunification, thc stability and instability of their work, the assumed life in the countryside, and migrant workers' hopes and plans for the future.

Music and film: The slogan of the band *New Worker Art Troupe* is: “Advocate with singing, safeguard rights through art”. Since its establishment on May 1st, 2002, the Troupe has performed over 500 times for migrant workers, reached audiences of over 100 thousand, issued 3 CDs, produced 2 theatre plays, 2 films and several documentary films.

The Culture and Art Festival of the new workers: With the support of Oxfam Hong Kong, the Migrant Workers' Home hosted *The First Art and Cultural Festival of Migrant Workers* from January 1 to January 3 in 2009. Migrant workers and relevant NGOs, university students, researchers and scholars from all over the country came to participate in the performances as well as the workshops and other activities. This has become a platform for migrant workers to create and exhibit their own culture. The slogan of the Festival is “Build our own stage, put on our own shows.”

Children's programs: Starting from 2007, with the support of its sponsors[2], the Migrant Workers' Home has carried out a series of Children programs, including drawing, photography, sports and games, as well as a young journalists program. These programs encourage migrant children to reflect on their lives as well as to voice their concerns. The magazinc, *The Voices of Migration* is especially designed to reach out to the migrant children.

2　The sponsors were PLAN international, Right to Play China, JP Morgan, Narada Foundation and Hilton Group China.

7　Die Kultur der neuen Arbeiter

Das Kunst- und Kulturmuseum der Wanderarbeiter: Im Jahr 2008 gründete das Migrant Workers' Home mit Unterstützung von Oxfam Hongkong ein Museum, das sich der Dokumentation der dreißigjährigen Geschichte von Chinas Wanderarbeitern widmet. 2009 eröffnete das Museum eine neue Ausstellung zum *Aufenthaltsstatus von Wanderarbeitern,* in der die Lebensbedingungen der Wanderarbeiter, das Problem der Familienzusammenführung; Sicherheiten und Unsicherheiten der Arbeitsplätze thematisiert wurden. Die Ausstellung präsentiert außerdem die Beziehungen der Wanderarbeiter zum früheren Landleben sowie deren Zukunftspläne.

Musik und Film: Das Motto der Band *Truppe der neuen Arbeiter* lautet: „Artikuliere dich durch Gesang, verteidige deine Rechte durch Kunst“. Seit ihrer Gründung im Mai 2002 kann die *Truppe der neuen Arbeiter* auf mehr als 500 Auftritte mit mehr als 100.000 Zuschauern zurückblicken. Die Musiker haben bereits drei CDs sowie zwei Theaterstücke und diverse Filme veröffentlicht.

Das *Festival der Kunst und Kultur der Wanderarbeiter:* Mit Unterstützung von Oxfam Hongkong richtete Migrant Workers' Home im Januar 2009 das mehrtägige *Festival der Kunst und Kultur der Wanderarbeiter* aus. Wanderarbeiter, Studenten, Forscher und Wissenschaftler aus dem ganzen Land beteiligten sich an den Aufführungen, Workshops und anderen Aktivitäten. Das Festival ist somit auch zu einer Plattform für Wanderarbeiter geworden. Dort können sie ihre eigene Kunst und Kultur ausstellen, getreu dem Motto des Festivals: „Wir errichten unsere eigene Bühne, produzieren unsere eigene Kunst.“

Kinderprogramm: Seit 2007 führt Migrant Workers' Home mit Unterstützung seiner Sponsoren[2] eine Reihe von Programmen für Kinder durch. Diese Mal-, Schreib- und Fotografiekurse, sowie das Sportangebot sollen das Selbstbewusstsein der Kinder stärken und sie ermutigen, ihr Leben zu reflektieren und ihre Interessen selbstbewusst auszudrücken. Die Zeitschrift *Die Stimmen der Migration* richtet sich speziell an diese Wanderarbeiterkinder.

2　Die Sponsoren waren PLAN international, Right to Play China, JP Morgan, Narada Foundation und Hilton Group China.

The entrance to the Community Activitiy Center which hosts: The Culture and Art Museum of Migrant Workers, the Workers' Cinema, the New Workers' Theatre Hall, the Workers' Library, 2010

Exhibition halls for *Thirty Years Migration* (2008–)

The Workers' Library

Exhibition hall for *Thirty Years Migration* (2008–)

Exhibition hall for *Migrant Workers Residential Status* (2009)

Exhibition hall for *Thirty Years History* (2008–)

Exhibition hall for migrant children (2008–)

Exhibition hall for workers' NGOs (2008–)

Exhibition hall for *Thirty Years Migration* (2008–)

Exhibition hall for migrant women (2008–)

All photos: Migrant Workers' Home 2008

The Second Fesitival for Migrant Children in Picun Village (2010)

The First Festival for Migrant Workers in Picun Village (2009)

8　资本全球化与中国新工人阶级的形成

8.1　移民工人对中国和世界经济的贡献

中国经济对世界经济的贡献率已从1978年的2%，上升到2008年的22%。2009年中国经济总量位居世界第三，有望在2010年超过日本，成为世界第二大经济体。2009年中国对世界经济增长的贡献超过50%，已位居世界第一。2009年中国出口总额首次赶超德国跃居全球第一。
根据联合国资料，我国已经逐渐成为世界制造业大国。我国制造业增加值占世界的份额由1995年的5.1%上升到2007年的11.4%.国务院研究室2006年发布《中国农民工调研报告》显示，移民工人数已占第二产业的58%，商业和餐饮业的53%，加工制造业的68%，建筑业的80%.换言之，如果没有移民工，超过一半的饭店要停业，近七成的生产厂家要关，近八成的大楼建不起来.
打工者的经济收入是支持农村生计的主要来源。根据国家统计局服务业调查中心在2006年10月所做的《农民工生活质量调查》显示,有一半的农民工把自己收入的一半寄（带）回了家乡。

8. The Globalization of Capital and the Making of the Chinese New Working Class

8.1 The contribution of the migrant workers to China's and the world economy

China's economic contribution to the world economy has increased from 2% in 1978 to 22% in 2008. China's economic output (GDP) in 2009 ranked third in the world. China's contribution to the world economic growth is more than 50%, making China the number one contributor. China's export surpassed Germany in 2009, making China the number one in export value in the world.
China has become a world manufacturing power. China's share of world manufacturing value increased from 5% in 1995 to 11% in 2007 as the data by the United Nations indicates. According to *The Research Report on China's Migrant Workers* by the State Council Research Office (2006), migrant workers account for 58% of the labor force in the secondary industry, 53% in the commerce and catering industry, 68% in the manufacture industry, and 80% in the construction industry. In other words, without migrant workers, more than half of the restaurants would close down, nearly seventy percent of manufacturing companies would shut, and nearly eighty percent of buildings could not be erected.
The repatriation of migrant workers' income to the countryside is a major source of income for rural villages. According to *The Survey on the Quality of Migrant Workers' Life* by The National Bureau of Statistics (2006), half of the migrant workers send approximately half of their income to their home villages.

8. Die Globalisierung der Kapitalmärkte und die Herausbildung einer neuen chinesischen Arbeiterklasse

8.1 Der Beitrag der Wanderarbeiter zur chinesischen und zur globalen Wirtschaft

Chinas Beitrag zur Weltwirtschaft hat sich von 2% im Jahr 1978 auf 22% in 2008 gesteigert. Chinas Bruttoinlandsprodukt war 2009 das dritthöchste der Welt. Chinas Beitrag zum globalen Wirtschaftswachstum ist mit über 50% an erster Stelle der Statistik. China exportierte in 2009 mehr als Deutschland, womit China zum Exportweltmeister wurde. China ist zu einer führenden Industrienation geworden, wie auch Zahlen der Vereinten Nationen bestätigen. Chinas Anteil am Wertzuwachs der weltweiten Produktion erhöhte sich von 5% im Jahr 1995 auf 11% in 2007.
Laut *Forschungsbericht über die Wanderarbeit in China* des Forschungsbüros des Staatsrates von 2006 sind 58% der Arbeitskräfte in der verarbeitenden Industrie, 53% in Handel und Gastronomie, 68% in der Fertigungsindustrie und 80% im Baugewerbe Wanderarbeiter. Man kann also sagen, dass ohne die Arbeitskraft der Wanderarbeiter mehr als die Hälfte der Restaurants sowie der Industriebetriebe schließen müsste und 80 Prozent aller Gebäude nicht errichtet werden könnten.
Der Rückfluss der Einkommen von Wanderarbeitern in ihre Heimatdörfer ist eine Haupteinnahmequelle für ländliche Gebiete. Laut der *Umfrage zur Lebensqualität von Wanderarbeitern* des Nationalen Amtes für Statistik von 2006 schickt die Hälfte der Wanderarbeiter etwa die Hälfte ihres Lohns in die Heimat.

8.2 资本全球化对中国的影响是

中国的改革开放和资本的全球化，使中国成为世界工厂，用廉价劳动力、低技术和低价格形成竞争优势，产生2亿多的新移民工群体。

一个中国的经济学家做了计算，我们出口一亿条牛仔裤，就可以换回来一架波音飞机。那个经济学家认为在中国现在的发展阶段，这个买卖很合算。但是，我们是否要考虑一下生产出一亿条牛仔裤的工人的生存和权益状况。资本在压迫工人，技术在资本的操控下也可以用来剥削工人。

8.2 The impact of capital globalization on China

China's reform and opening up, in line with the capital globalization, has transformed China into a world factory, which takes advantage of the cheap Chinese labor force, including a majority of more than 200 million migrant workers.

One Chinese economist has done a calculation: the value of exporting 100 million pair of jeans is equal to that of a Boeing aircraft. That economist believes that this deal is very cost-effective in China's current stage of development. However, such logic may not stand should we think about the interests and rights of the workers who produce the jeans. Capital exploits workers, and technologies under control of capital can also be used to exploit workers.

8.2 Die Auswirkungen der Globalisierung der Kapitalmärkte auf China

Die Reformen und der Öffnungsprozess Chinas zur Weltwirtschaft sowie die Globalisierung der Kapitalmärkte haben das Land in eine globale Fabrik verwandelt, die billige chinesische Arbeitskräfte, unter denen die 200 Millionen Wanderarbeiter die Mehrheit bilden, zu ihrem Vorteil nutzt.

Ein chinesischer Wirtschaftswissenschaftler hat errechnet, dass der Wert unserer 100 Millionen Exportjeans dem Wert eines einzigen Flugzeuges entspricht. Diese Gegenüberstellung visualisiert die Rentabilität der chinesischen Textilindustrie in der gegenwärtigen Situation. Diese Ausmaße wären wohl kaum zu erzielen, wenn wir die Rechte der Arbeiter berücksichtigen, die diese Jeans in den chinesischen Fabriken produzieren. Das Kapital dient der Ausbeutung der Arbeiter und unter der Kontrolle des Kapitals können auch Technologien zur Ausbeutung der Arbeiter verwendet werden.

8.3 中国新工人阶级的形成

资本的文化和中国的历史在影响着中国人的思维。当和中国很多中产阶级谈论打工群体的困境、愤怒和抗争的时候，他们都很回避，认为可以谈问题，但是不要谈阶级。这就是我们的现实：明明中国已经出现了阶级分化，但是很多人不能面对

国务院在2006年3月公布了《关于解决农民工问题的若干意见》，文件重点指出：移民工是我国改革开放和工业化、城镇化进程中涌现的一支新型劳动产业大军。2010年中央一号文件提出：新生代打工群体已经成为新工人的主体.所谓新生代移民工，主要是指80后和90后的打工者。目前，这一群体约占整个外出打工群体人数的60%。

在美国《时代》周刊的年度人物评选中，作为一个群体的“中国工人”以亚军身份上榜。对这个事情，各界的反应不同，很多人认为这是美国主流媒体对中国工人对世界经济发展和抵抗金融危机的贡献的高度认可。但是我们也听到了工人这样的声音：“听到这个消息我特别郁闷，尤其看着眼前工友疲惫的身影。这是给我们一个高帽戴，让我们自以为是英雄，好更加努力地为老板卖命。我特别气愤。”

8.3 The making of China's new working class

The culture of capital and the history of China are influencing Chinese people's thinking. Middle-class people consciously avoid talking about the life of the poor, including their difficulties and their anger. This is the reality: China cannot face up to the fact that there is class stratification in China.

The State Council in March 2006 announced *A number of opinions on resolving the issue of migrant workers,* which stressed: "Migrant workers have become a new industrial labor force that is making great contributions to China's reform and opening up, industrialization and urbanization process". In early 2010, the central government issued its No. 1 Paper, which indicates: The new generation of migrant workers make up the majority of the migrant workers. Appropriate measures should be adopted to tackle their problems.

Chinese workers ranked second in the runners-up for the *Time's* person of the year 2009. By selecting the Chinese group, the magazine is actually highlighting the role of the Chinese economy in helping the world economy step out of the crisis. However, we have also heard such voice of a migrant worker: "I feel so depressed after I heard this news, especially when I saw worn-out workers walking by in front of me at mid-night. They gave us a 'title' so that we would think that we were heroes, so that we would sell ourselves with all our efforts. I feel very angry."

8.3 Die Entstehung von Chinas neuer Arbeiterklasse

Die Kultur des Kapitals und die Geschichte Chinas beeinflussen das Denken des chinesischen Volkes. Die Mittelschicht vermeidet bewusst, über das Leben der Armen, über ihre Probleme und ihre Wut zu sprechen. So sieht die Realität aus: China verdrängt die Tatsache, dass die Bevölkerung in eine Klassengesellschaft aufgeteilt ist.

Im März 2006 verkündete der Staatsrat jedoch einige *Ansätze zur Förderung der Wanderarbeiter.* Es wurde betont: „Wanderarbeiter sind eine neue Kraft auf dem industriellen Arbeitsmarkt. Sie leisten einen bedeutenden Beitrag sowohl zu den Reformen und der Öffnung Chinas als auch zum Industrialisierungs- und Urbanisierungsprozess.“ Anfang 2010 veröffentlichte die Zentralregierung ihre Ausarbeitung Nummer 1, in der erklärt wird, dass geeignete Maßnahmen ergriffen werden sollen, um die Probleme der jüngeren Generation anzugehen, da die Mehrheit der Wanderarbeiter eben dieser Generation angehöre.

Außerdem wählte das *Time Magazine* die chinesischen Arbeiter bei ihrer Wahl zur Person des Jahres 2009 auf den zweiten Platz. Mit dieser Geste sollte die Aufmerksamkeit auf diese Personengruppe und ihre Rolle in der chinesischen Wirtschaft bei der Bewältigung der Finanzkrise gelenkt werden. Allerdings kommentierte ein Wanderarbeiters diesen Titel wie folgt: „Diese Nachricht hat mich unglaublich deprimiert, besonders als ich um Mitternacht vollkommen erschöpfte Arbeiter an mir vorbeiziehen sah. Sie haben uns diesen ‚Titel‘ verliehen, damit wir uns wie Helden fühlen und uns mit all unserer Kraft verkaufen. Ich bin sehr wütend.“

9. 工人的故事

9.1 曹秀芝

努力奋斗

- 女，一九六八年出生，河北人；
- 一九八九年来京
- 一九九零年：在包工队板砖，每天挣十元钱；
- 一九九一年——一九九二年：在纺布厂车间做工，每月伍佰元；
- 一九九三年——一九九六年：在北京地铁车辆段停车库做清洁工（洗涮地铁），每月三百元；
- 一九九三年———九九六年：兼职给包工队做饭；
- 一九九六年下半年：做小时工，三小时十元钱；
- 一九九七年三月十八到今：在北京青年报发行处小红帽发行部做发行员，现任发行分点主管，一年到头没有休息。

最大的心愿：能有一天休息！

9. Short biographies of some individual migrant workers

9.1 Cao Xiuzhi—*Strive for the future*

- Cao was born in 1968 in Hebei Province.
- In 1989 she came to Beijing to work there on a construction site for one year. She earned 10 yuan a day (about 1 euro).
- From 1991 to 1992, she worked as a textile factory worker making 500 yuan (54 euro) a month.
- From 1993 to 1996 she works as a cleaner for the Beijing subway and making 300 yuan (33 euro) a month; while doing this part-time job she was cooking for a construction team on a construction site.
- Second half of 1996 she worked as a day worker making 10 yuan (1 euro) for every three-hour work.
- In 1997 she started a job as a delivery person for Beijing Youth Newspaper, then she became the chief of a newspaper distribution station. She has to work every day throughout the year.

My wish: "I really want to take a break, even just for one day."

9. Kurzbiographien einzelner Wanderarbeiter

9.1 Cao Xiuzhi – *Kampf um die Zukunft*

- Cao wurde 1968 in der nördlichen Provinz Hebei geboren.
- 1989 ging sie nach Peking, um dort für ein Jahr auf einer Baustelle für einen Tageslohn von 10 Yuan (ca. 1 Euro) zu arbeiten.
- Von 1991 bis 1992 war sie als Textilarbeiterin mit einem Monatslohn von 500 Yuan (54 Euro) angestellt.
- Von 1993 bis 1996 arbeitete sie als Reinigungskraft in der U-Bahn von Peking mit einem Monatslohn von 300 Yuan (33 Euro); nebenbei kochte sie auf einer Baustelle für die dort tätigen Bauarbeiter.
- In der zweiten Hälfte des Jahres 1996 arbeitete sie als Tagelöhnerin für 10 Yuan (ca. 1 Euro) für drei Stunden tägliche Arbeit.
- 1997 begann sie dann als Zustellerin für die Jugendzeitung Peking. Seit sie bei der Zeitung als Leiterin einer Vertriebsstelle angestellt ist, arbeitet sie das ganze Jahr über sieben Tage in der Woche.

Mein Wunsch: „Eine Pause, sei es auch nur für einen Tag."

9.2 陈玉英

女，一九七四年出生，重庆人；

- 一九八九年——一九九零年：到深圳打工，没有找到合适的工作，回家；
- 一九九零年——一九九一年：再次到深圳，在一家小型玩具厂工作；
- 一九九一年——一九九三年：在深圳致丽玩具厂工作；
- 一九九三年十一月十九日：深圳致丽玩具厂发生火灾，小英深受重伤；
- 一九九三年十一月十九日——一九九四年七月：在深圳某医院一边治疗一边学习；
- 一九九四年七月——一九九七年：回家，一边康复一边学习；
- 一九九七年——一九九八年：做手术，参加无线电培训学习；
- 一九九八年——二零零零年：开始关注并支持致丽工伤工友；
- 二零零零年——二零零三年：开始自学法律专业知识；
- 二零零二年五月：发起创办"重庆忠县自强服务站"为工伤工友及残疾朋友至今；

最大的心愿：把自强服务站办好办下去，为更多工友服务！

9.2 Chen Yuying—*Road of self-reliance*

- Chen was born in 1974, in Chongqing Municipality.
- In 1989/1990 she moved to Shenzhen but failed to find a job in the city und returned home.
- In 1990/1991 Chen went to Shenzhen again and worked in a small toy factory.
- Then she worked in Zhili Toy Factory for 2 years.
- On November 19, 1993 Zhili Toy Factory caught a big fire, which caused 87 deaths and 51 injuries. Yuying was seriously injured.
- Until July 1994, she was hospitalized und took the time to read and learn things by herself.
- After returning home for recovery, she continued "self-learning" for the next 3 years.
- In 1997 she received surgery and later joined a radio engineering training.
- From 1998 to 2000 she started to pay attention to what happened to her injured fellow workers after the big fire.
- In May, 2002 she founded the *Self-Reliance Service Station* in Zhouxian County of Chongqing Municipality, which provides services for injured workers and the physically disabled.
- From 2000 to 2003 she educated herself about the law.

My wish: "To optimize the *Self-Reliance Service Station* and to support the migrant workers."

9.2 Chen Yuying – *Der Weg des Selbstvertrauens*

- Chen Yuying wurde 1974 in der Stadt Chongqing geboren.
- Sie zog 1989/90 nach Shenzhen. Da sie keinen Job fand, kehrte sie zurück in ihre Heimat.
- 1990/91 ging sie erneut nach Shenzhen und arbeitete in einer kleinen Spielzeugfabrik.
- Von 1991 bis 1993 arbeitete sie in der Spielzeugfabrik „Zhili".
- Am 19. November 1993 kamen bei einem Großbrand in der Spielzeugfabrik „Zhili" 87 Menschen ums Leben und 51 Personen wurden verletzt. Yuying gehörte zu den Schwerverletzten.
- Während ihres folgenden achtmonatigen Krankenhausaufenthaltes hat sie viel gelesen und bildete sich autodidaktisch weiter.
- Von 1994 bis 1997 verbrachte sie die Zeit ihrer Genesung damit, sich im Selbststudium weiterzubilden.
- Nach einer letzten Operation infolge ihrer Verletzungen machte sie von 1997 bis 1998 eine Ausbildung als Radiotechnikerin.
- In den folgenden zwei Jahren erreichten sie immer wieder tragische Geschichten ihrer Arbeitskollegen nach dem Großbrand in der Fabrik.
- Im Mai 2002 gründete sie das *Haus der Unterstützung und des Selbstvertrauens* im Stadtbezirk Zhouxian der Großstadt Chongqing, die verletzte Arbeiter und Invaliden unterstützt.
- Von 2000 bis 2003 beschäftigte sie sich im Selbststudium mit juristischen Fragestellungen

Mein Wunsch: „Das *Haus der Unterstützung und des Selbstvertrauens* weiter ausbauen, um immer mehr Wanderarbeitern helfen zu können."

9.3 马振的故事

- 马振出生于1985年。
- 1999年，小马开始外出打工，跟随一个同乡的亲戚去一个砖窑打工。之后，他曾到过天津塘沽，河北唐山，山西大同，浙江温州，福建福鼎，山西河津等地，做过建筑工人，打过铁，下过矿井，配过化肥，搬过水泥。
- 2003年，他跟随表弟来到唐山一个建筑工地打工。每天披星戴月夜以继日的干活，却每天只拿到18元工资，半年只干了4个月的活。除了车费和生活费，只挣了1500元钱。小马就是带着这1500元回家了，准备办婚事。
- 2005年，考虑到刚刚办完婚事，家里需要用钱，经由一个老乡的介绍，他不顾生命危险，下到300多米深的井下采矿。那是一段不堪回首的日子，一米七七的小伙，在低矮的矿井里干活，是很难直起腰板的，井下随时都有塌方的危险。碰到下雨天，井下更加危险，上面警铃一旦响起，井下的工人必须马上争相撤离。更危险的是，由于都是黑矿井，都不按照规定操作，两个矿井之间不过一墙之隔，有时候，那边爆破这边的工人在井下都能感觉到强烈的震颤，抖落的矿石随时可能危及生命。
- 2006年，小马来到温州仓兰，在一家工厂工作，起早贪黑的拼命干活，却无法拿到属于自己的血汗钱，无奈之下，他借口自己肚子痛需要上医院，才勉强得到老板给的20元钱，小马拿着这20元钱开始了下一个阶段的漂泊。
- 2009年，小马和妻子来到北京皮村。小马当搬运工，妻子在一个幼儿园当厨师。 女儿在老家由爷爷奶奶照看 。

我的梦想是做一个老板，为了这个梦想，我要拼命努力，无论多苦多累我都能默默忍受。我希望通过当老板来赢得身份的改变和社会的尊重。

9.3 Ma Zhen

- Ma Zhen was born in 1985,
- In 1999, he went to work at a brick mill; he was only 14 years old then. In the later years, he worked in Tianjin, Tangshan of Hebei, Datong of Shanxi, Wenzhou of Zhejiang, Fuding of Fujian, etc.
- In 2003, he worked on a construction site for a daily wage of 18 yuan (2 euros). He only had 1500 yuan (165 euros) left to bring home after half a year work;
- In 2005, he got married. Being short of money, he went to work in a mine. The depth of the mine was 300 meters. One had to bend to work inside, for the channel was not wide enough. The miners were constantly in danger of losing their lives when there was a heavy rain or when explosives went off nearby in other mines.
- In 2006, he worked in Canglan of Wenzhou. The work was tough and he was not paid on time. In the end, he lied to his boss saying that he was very sick and asked for 20 yuan to see a doctor. He left Canglan with only 20 Yuan in his pocket.
- In 2009, he worked as a porter in Picun Village of Beijing. His wife joined him and worked as a cook in a kindergarten. Their daughter staid behind in the countryside with the grandparents.

My wish: "I want to become a big manager. For achieving this dream, I am making all my efforts. I don't mind hardship and tough life as long as I would become a manager to win the respect of the society and to change my status."

9.3 Ma Zhen

- Ma Zhen wurde 1985 geboren.
- 1999 nahm er im Alter von 14 Jahren eine Arbeit in einer Ziegelei auf. In den folgenden Jahren arbeitete er in verschiedenen Städten. Er zog von der Hafenstadt Tianjin in die Industriestadt Tangshan in der Provinz Hebei. Weitere Stationen waren Datong in der Provinz Shanxi, Wenzhou in der Provinz Zhejiang und Fuding in der Provinz Fujian.
- 2003 arbeitete er auf einer Baustelle für einen Tageslohn von 18 Yuan (ca. 2 Euro). Nach einem halben Jahr Arbeit hatte er nur 1.500 Yuan (165 Euro) für seine Familie zurücklegen können.
- 2005 heiratete er. Da das Geld knapp war, suchte er sich Arbeit in einer Mine. Im Innern der 300 Meter tiefen Mine musste Ma in gebückter Haltung arbeiten, denn der Grubengang war nicht hoch genug. Die Minenarbeiter befanden sich in ständiger Lebensgefahr, da die Mine bei starkem Regen oder bei Sprengungen in nahe gelegenen Minen einsturzgefährdet war.
- 2006 arbeitete er in der Stadt Wenzhou. Da Ma trotz harter Arbeit seine Bezahlung nicht pünktlich erhielt, täuschte er seinem Vorgesetzten eine Krankheit vor, um 20 Yuan (ca. 2 Euro) für den Arztbesuch zu erhalten. Mit diesem wenigen Geld flüchtete er schließlich.
- Seit 2009 arbeitet Ma als Pförtner im Dorf Picun bei Peking. Seine Frau zog nach und arbeitet als Köchin in einem Kindergarten. Ihre gemeinsame Tochter blieb auf dem Land bei den Großeltern.

Mein Wunsch: „Ich möchte mein eigener Chef werden. Entbehrungen und Anstrengungen nehme ich für die Verwirklichung meines Traumes auf mich. Ich möchte von der Gesellschaft respektiert werden und meinen Status verbessern."

Exhibition view at IG Metall, Berlin, October 8, 2010 – January 2, 2011

Installation view at Museu Reina Sofia Madrid, May 12 – September 6, 2010. Photo: courtesy Zhibin Lin

Installation view at Museo Nacional de Etnografía y Folklore in La Paz, February 22 – April 30, 2011. Photo: courtesy Zhibin Lin

THE MAKING OF THE CHINESE NEW WORKING CLASS THIRTY YEARS OF MIGRATION

An exhibition by the Culture and Art Museum
of Migrant Workers Beijing

Installation views, MINI/Goethe-Institut Curatorial Residencies Ludlow 38, New York, July 14 – September 4, 2011

劳动最光荣
Trabajar es glorioso
Labor is glorious
KONG YIK CO.
ROCO GC CORP.
STOP

集錦香食品公司
電話:212-777-5881
917-882-8687
38 LUDLOW ST.
拉露街
Architectural
40
SPACE
2129645578
CITY-GATES
939-9700
我们的世界
Our World
我们的梦想
Our Dream
Conclusion
Conclusion
GOETHE INSTITUT
LUDLOW

Workers Rights
Participación política
Political Participation
According to the Chinese law, migrant workers are only eligible to participate in the election at the place of their household registration in their hometown. In this way, they are excluded from the political participation in cities where they work and live. In March 2008, for the first time three migrant workers were elected as National People's Congress representatives.
Seguridad social
Social Security

Derechos de los trabajadores
Workers' Rights
Participación política
Political Participation
Seguridad social
Social Security

algunas empresas.
ways: 60.37% of the workers were paid on a monthly
.78% received their wages on time. In 2004 survey, the
wages to migrant workers. In 2009 survey, of those who
13% were owed wages. Of those who returned home as
rticipación política
olitical Participation
la legislación china los trabajadores migrantes sólo pueden
en el lugar donde se encuentra empadronada su familia, en
ueblos. Por consiguiente, quedan excluidos de la participación
ca en las ciudades donde viven y trabajan.
arzo de 2008 se eligió por primera vez a tres trabajadores
ntes como diputados de la Asamblea Popular Nacional.
rding to the Chinese law, migrant workers are only eligible
articipate in the election at the place of their household
ration in their hometown. In this way, they are excluded
the political participation in cities where they work and live.
arch 2008, for the first time three migrant workers were
ed as National People's Congress representatives.

劳动节大声唱!
新公民儿童文化艺术节
Treinta años de historia de la migración
Mapping of the Thirty Years History of Migration
225,000,000
210,000,000
Construction tools

herramienta para pintar
Paint tool
herramientas de minería
Shelfworker tools
herramientas de carpintería
Woodworking tools
herramienta de construcción
Construction tools

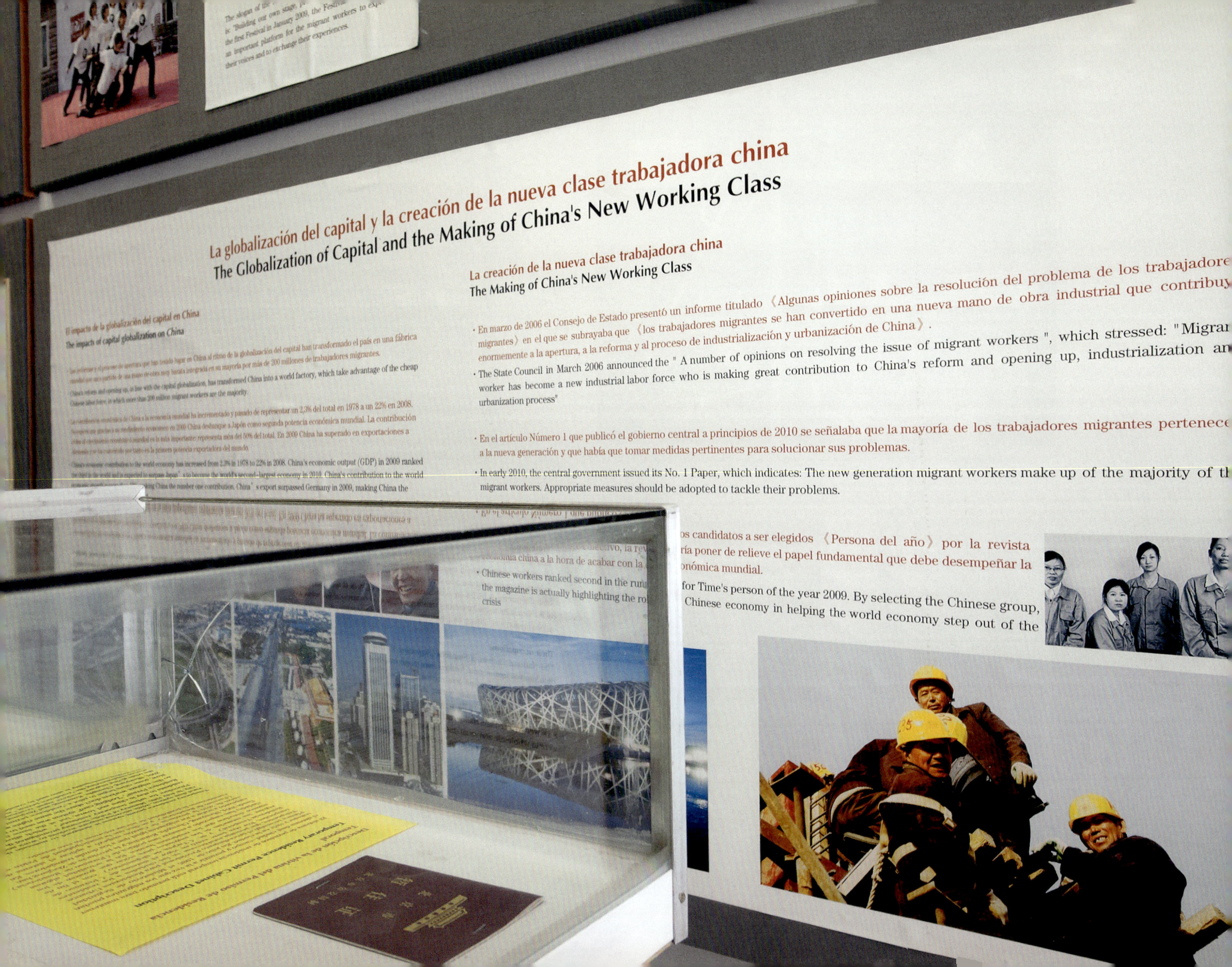
La globalización del capital y la creación de la nueva clase trabajadora china
The Globalization of Capital and the Making of China's New Working Class
El impacto de la globalización del capital en China
The impacts of capital globalization on China
La creación de la nueva clase trabajadora china
The Making of China's New Working Class
• En marzo de 2006 el Consejo de Estado presentó un informe titulado 《Algunas opiniones sobre la resolución del problema de los trabajadores migrantes》 en el que se subrayaba que 《los trabajadores migrantes se han convertido en una nueva mano de obra industrial que contribuy enormemente a la apertura, a la reforma y al proceso de industrialización y urbanización de China》.
• The State Council in March 2006 announced the " A number of opinions on resolving the issue of migrant workers ", which stressed: "Migrant worker has become a new industrial labor force who is making great contribution to China's reform and opening up, industrialization an urbanization process"
• En el artículo Número 1 que publicó el gobierno central a principios de 2010 se señalaba que la mayoría de los trabajadores migrantes pertenece a la nueva generación y que había que tomar medidas pertinentes para solucionar sus problemas.
• In early 2010, the central government issued its No. 1 Paper, which indicates: The new generation migrant workers make up of the majority of th migrant workers. Appropriate measures should be adopted to tackle their problems.
os candidatos a ser elegidos 《Persona del año》 por la revista
ría poner de relieve el papel fundamental que debe desempeñar la
onómica mundial.
• Chinese workers ranked second in the
for Time's person of the year 2009. By selecting the Chinese group,
Chinese economy in helping the world economy step out of the
crisis

EXIT
60,000,000
20,000,000
1978, Reformas y ap
1978, Reform and open
Dificil de mig
Difficult to mig
1978

laws and regulations showcase
打工纪事（组诗）
通讯

TOSHIBA

劳动最光荣
五湖四海皆朋友
天下打工是一家
本厂急招
13266870324
第2届

五湖四海皆朋友
本厂急招
13266870324
13266870324
诚聘
内部直聘
内部直聘
户提保
工人致敬

尊严
劳动最光荣
Labor is Glorious
第2届
新工人文化艺术节
2010
庚寅年
虎
新工人社区
天下打工是一家
HOT MASSAGE FOOTBATH
H-203B
功能

第一届打工文化艺术节
尊严
Dignity
中国·皮村 China · Picun Village
第2届
The Second
新工人文化艺术节
New Worker Art and Cultural Festival
展现打工文化风貌
Present New Workers' Culture
倡导劳动价值尊重
Show Respect to the Value of Labor
音乐
Music
电影
Film
戏剧
Theatre
诗歌
Poem
展览
Exhibition
论坛
Forum
联欢
Party
赶集
Market
工作坊
Workshop
研讨
Seminar
劳动最光荣
Labor is Glorious
2008
The Third 第3届 新工人文化艺术节
New Worker Art and Cultural Festival
展现打工文化风貌 倡导劳动价值尊重
音乐戏剧诗歌电影展览论坛工作坊
Music Theatre Poetry Film Show Exhibition Forum Workshop
www.dashengchang.org.cn
www.chengbiancun.com
2010
庚寅年
虎
新工人社区
五湖四海皆朋友
天下打工是一家

尊严
第2届
新工人文化艺术节
新工人文化艺术节
s Glorious
2010
庚寅年
虎
新工人社区
五湖四海皆朋友
天下打工是一家
HOT MASSAGE FOOTBATH
H-2038
功能

DDHTV
大伙来到这里求个发展
here seeking for a better

京華
洗涤灵
复方胃蛋白酶颗粒
重庆佳辰生物工程有限公司
雅特
多功能
玻璃净
Multifunctional Glass Cleaner

工 社区
天下打工是一家

Texts

ELLEN DAVID FRIEDMAN AND ZHIBIN LIN IN CONVERSATION

The exhibition at MINI / Goethe-Institut Curatorial Residencies Ludlow 38 on 38 Ludlow St., New York opened with a conversation between Zhibin Lin, research co-ordinator of the Culture and Art Museum of Migrant Workers, and Ellen David Friedman, a union organizer and labor educator living and working in the U.S. and China.

ZHIBIN LIN: The exhibit we are opening here tonight has traveled, if not around the world, to many parts of the world as it was part of an exhibition titled *Principle Potosí*. This exhibition has invited more than twenty artists from around the world, from Europe, from Latin America, and our project from China. Potosí is a city in Bolivia where the Spanish had stolen silver over a period of more than 150 years—from early 16th century to mid 17th century. Then this is how the laborers, the Indians there, were exploited and how the capital and gun power ruled the world 500 years ago. The idea of *Principle Potosí* says that this principle has been lasting until today. So even now you see what is happening in China, maybe also in the Unites States, that capital rules and laborers are exploited. We have put together this exhibition on the ocassion of the *Principle Potosí* exhibition. The reason why we were invited to this exhibition is that China passed 30 years of internal migration witnessing the same principle. China adopted the reform and opening-up policy in 1978. The official mainstream version on China's past 30-year history is more about how China has made an economic miracle and become the world's factory. However, this is just one side of the story. Little attention was given to who made this possible. It is the migrant workers who contributed to this whole process. By establishing a Culture and Art Museum of Migrant Workers in Beijing, we want to show the other side of the story. We collected items from across China that the workers donated, items like their work uniforms, working tools, their residential permit, salary slips, letters, etc. We have rented an abandoned factory and then set up this museum. The museum is one of the projects run by a non-profit organization based in Beijing called Migrant Workers' Home, where I work as a researcher.

It is estimated that there are now about 300 million migrant workers who have come to work in the Chinese cities from the countryside. And these people, especially the new generation of migrant workers, are lost in between the countryside and the city, and they are lost in the city because it is hard for them to stay in the city, and they can't go back to the countryside either. The reasons why it is difficult for them to go back are: first, agricultural income is very low mainly due to limited area of land that serves to make a living on agricultural production; secondly, many young migrant workers have never done any farming work, don't want to do farming work, and have become used to urban life. So this is what is going on in China. Our organization was established in 2002 by a group of young musicians who are also migrant workers themselves, and they started with singing songs, composing songs for the workers on the construction site, in the restaurants. It was like a big party for the workers. But then after the party, they wondered what to do next. We can't just sing songs. Even if songs are powerful, they are not enough. My colleagues published their first CD album and made 75000 RMB (approximately $11500). With this money they founded a school for migrant children, who do not have equal access to public schools. In 2005 we started to open second-hand shops to reduce the workers' living cost and also to use them as windows of interaction with the communities; now the museum; and we also have a training center, and various training programs, including computer repair, computer software, legal training, social work training, etc. So this is what we do in China. Now I would like to invite Ellen to hear her views about our exhibition and her experience in China.

ELLEN DAVID FRIEDMAN: I would just like to tell two short stories to give a little bit of a vivid outline to this 300 million strong migrant workforce that Zhibin has described and illustrated very vividly and carefully in this exhibit. In the Western media, if you pay attention at all to the issues of workers in China, you are left with this idea of a highly exploited, productive, disciplined, hard working and stoic group of people who will work endless hours, are forced to do overtime, are working for sub-minimum wage, but are docile, passive, and have not been resisting the exploitation. But in China every year there are at least 100,000 strikes, and not a single one of those strikes are called by the trade union. All of those strikes are wildcat strikes. And workers organize and defend themselves everyday under these severe economic conditions. They are organizing in some of the ways that you can see here to create a life, which is a tolerable life. In the rest of the industrialized world we pay attention to China, in part, because it is where the race to the bottom has been going for the last 30 years. And as Germany has de-industrialized, more slowly than the United States, but as the United States has deindustrialized very rapidly, this is where the work has gone. It is not that the Chinese workers have taken our jobs; it is that the American capitalists took their money and sent it to China to create these jobs. They will always go wherever the wages are the lowest.

I want to tell a quick story about what happened last spring. I teach every year at Sun Yat-sen University in Guangzhou, which is really the center of the industrial machine that has been powering China's tremendous economic rise in the last 30 years. Last spring there was a horrendous story that caught the media's attention about a factory compound in Shenzhen, just south of Guangzhou called Foxconn, the largest export electronics supply manufacturer in the world. They employ a million workers in China of which there are about 400,000 workers in 17 factories in Shenzhen. The media started to report last spring that there was a string of suicides taking place. Young workers, average age 19 years old, were jumping off buildings in this factory compound where they live in dormitories, and eat in canteens. It came as a surprise to many people that the media actually carried this story and was allowed to continue carrying it without being censored. You could just feel this discussion beginning, as people tried to contemplate: Is this the cost of our growth as an economic world power? Is this the price that we are paying? This second generation of migrant workers most of whom have completed high school, the great majority of whom are literate, have ambitions, have hopes for a family and a job, but they saw that capitalism with Chinese characteristics, as we say, was presenting no future for them. They could not imagine themselves in a life beyond this dreadful situation in the factory. Suicide seemed like the only option for them. And there were two-dozen suicides in the course of just about two months. So people, as they were beginning to think about this and whether China should be reconsidering its cheap labor policy, the second story broke in the news, and that was the beginning of the most important, the most militant, the most powerful strike wave that has ever happened in China's history, excluding probably the great Shanghai strikes in 1920. A group of young migrant workers, from vocational schools, average age 19 or 20, shut down a Honda transmission parts plant, just south of Guangzhou. Most of the strikes in China are defensive demands, just saying: We want to be paid, we want to be paid proper overtime, we want the temperature in the factory floor to be brought down, we want you to turn the air conditioning on so we are not broiling to death while we are working. But they made an

Exhibition opening and conversation between Zhibin Lin (left) and
Ellen David Friedman (right, from behind) outside 38 Ludlow Street in New York

aggressive demand, which was that they wanted their wages doubled because these teenagers had learned how to use the Internet, and in their free time they did some research and they saw how profitable Honda was. They also saw that workers doing their same job in other parts of the world were making, not only twice, but 50 times as much as they were making. They made a second demand, which was they wanted to democratize, to reform the union because the trade union in China is not really what we call a workers organization; it is an organization of the state, its job is to manage the workforce and not to represent the workforce. And this started a strike wave that lasted for the next several months. All Honda plants were shut down for two weeks. Three days later a strike started up in a Toyota parts plant and they shut down Toyota production in the entire country for about 10 days. One year later, wages in the car-manufacturing sector, which is huge and growing rapidly in China, have in fact doubled in South China. The labor movement started 150 years ago in the UK in response to the industrial revolution there, and then moved onto the European continent. It then moved to the United States a hundred years ago, and built itself up out of the blood, sweat, and tears of industrial workers just like the *Nong Min Gong*, the migrant workforce in China under conditions of incredible exploitation, where it is clear to the workers that vast profit is being made enriching someone, but just not them. Under those conditions, consciousness is beginning to form. I think that the choice of the name of the exhibit is correct, *The Making of the Chinese New Working Class*. It is just being born now, and I think of this as a birth announcement. I want to thank Zhibin for the work in her NGO to create this, the creativity, the audacity and courage to do it.

Audience: Are there any conflicts between the old working class and migrant workers?

ZL: From my observation, the situation in the South and the North is not the same different but one common phenomenon is that the locals "welcome" the migrants to rent the housing so that the locals can make money. In the village in Beijing where I work and live, one local family may rent out 20 rooms, and for each room they can make about 200 RMB a month, which is about $35. It is similar in the South. Having said this, I didn't mean this sort of "welcoming" is positive. The locals and the migrants are not integrated, and the migrants are treated as the second class.

EDF: One of the things that are happening in Beijing now actually is that there are these phenomena that are called 'villages in the city' which is where migrant workers come, live and congregate. There is a developing attitude; we might even say it is a racist form of racism. I certainly see it in Guangzhou where I live, where local urban residents think that the crime comes from the migrants, e.g. sexually transmitted disease. And gambling is a serious problem, which is associated very often with migrant workers. So one thing that was happening last winter is the gating of some of these villages in the city and some of them are putting up walls and gates. They are even establishing a curfew and saying that people have to be in by a certain time and then the gates are locked, which is very serious. There was a three-day riot in Guangzhou that took place one week ago.[1] Now there are often violent little conflicts between police and citizens. The story was that a policeman handled a pregnant migrant worker who was selling on the street roughly, he pushed her down, some people responded, and it started a riot that lasted for three days. The government couldn't stop it, even though they brought in a lot of military and police forces. One of the theories I have heard about why this has gone on is because there is so much underlying tension between urban residents and migrant workers.

Audience: Could you explain the difference between the urban workers and the migrant workers who through the home registration policy are not allowed to establish permanent residence in the cities?

ZL: Maybe we are the only country in the world that has this so-called *Household Registration System*. So you are registered in the place where you were born and you are bound to that place. First of all, there are two categories for the whole population, either you are a farmer or you are an urban citizen. For instance, if you come to work in Beijing, but your registration is in the other province then you are only given a so-called temporary residential permit, means you are not considered as a local resident, even if you have worked and lived there for a long time. Many of my friends in the village where I work have been living there for 10, even 20 years, but they are still given temporary residential permits. Somebody joked about it: "I've been temporarily living here for 20 years." This is the *Household Registration System*. It is like building walls that categorize people into different classes. For those who are from the countryside, even though they are not farming, they are still labeled as farmers and thus not treated equally. That is why in China they are called "peasant workers". We think you can't be both, you are either a peasant or you are a worker. This terminology is a way to discriminate against, to say, "Since you are registered, labeled as a peasant, you shouldn't be treated as a worker."

Audience: In relation to this event that just happened in Guangzhou, I heard that the culmination of it was that it was agreed to build a migrant workers museum in Guangzhou. What do you think about that and do you worry that this notion of a migrant workers museum can be used to just diffuse the situation?

ZL: Maybe Ellen can comment, but I just wanted to make a correction. The name of the museum is translated into English as "migrant workers museum," but in Chinese it literally means "peasant workers museum".

EDF: I think we would say that this is cosmetic. And as compared to the museum that was started by the group that Zhibin works with, which is a grassroots organization of migrant workers to actually create a space and a platform for self-respect, this is a typical move by the government to try and appear as if they wish to honor the workers and create a sense of harmonious society. But I think in general the reaction from workers would be cynical, they will think this museum is being built instead of actually creating the opportunities for them to be equal citizens.

1 The riot I refer to took place on June 10, 11 & 12, 2011 in the Zengcheng district of Guangzhou.

Maspeth, Queens, NY, 2011 (Photo: Marty Kirchner)

MIGRANT WORKERS IN CHINA AND IMMIGRANT WORKERS IN THE UNITED STATES

By Marty Kirchner

In conjunction with *The Making of the Chinese New Working Class*, a series of events were planned to help contextualize the exhibition for a New York audience. The presentations and discussions at these events focused on current efforts by migrant workers, both in China and the United States, who are organizing to defend their rights. In China it is estimated that over 150 million people—or about half the population of the United States—are migrant workers. Having migrated from the rural provinces to work long hours under extremely harsh and unsafe conditions in industrial compounds like Foxconn Technology Group, these low-wage workers are denied the right to organize, are forced to work an excessive amount of overtime, are exposed to dust and occupational diseases, and are subjected to military-style management. In the Unites States, studies have exposed the systematic and routine violation of employment and labor law in core sectors of the economy. Particularly for low-wage workers, many of color and foreign-born, workplace violations are severe and widespread. According to labor scholars Janice Fine and Jennifer Gordon, "A recent study found that 26 percent of low-wage workers in the nation's three largest cities suffered minimum-wage violations in the week prior to the survey, and more than 76 percent of low-wage workers who labored more than forty hours in the prior week were not paid according to overtime laws." When employers violate the law, almost no enforcement gets taken. Instead, workers are often either ignored or even threatened by the very government agencies that have been set up to protect them.

In both China and the United States, while unsafe and inhumane working conditions have become standard practice in many industries, local residents express open hostility to the presence of new migrants. Recently in Guangdong province, where many Chinese migrant workers live, conflicts have been escalating between local residents and migrant workers. According to the China Labour Bulletin, in one such conflict in June 2011, local security guards in the district of Zengcheng "pushed a pregnant migrant street vendor to the ground inciting thousands of angry migrant workers to take to the streets." In the meantime, federal programs in the U.S. like the misnamed "Secure Communities" and the spread of harsh anti-immigrant state legislation continue to further marginalize immigrant families. In states like Arizona, Georgia, and Alabama, laws are being passed with the express aim of creating misery and panic for unauthorized immigrants. Over the last several decades, as U.S. society has experienced a steady decline of participation in civic, social, and political life—the work of citizenship—it is deeply troubling to witness the growing intolerance and scapegoating of noncitizen immigrants living and working in the United States. Countless studies have shown the significant economic contribution immigrant workers make to the U.S. economy. In both the United States and China, those who perform the bulk of the hard labor on which we all depend are legally excluded from the right to vote, and from any right to political representation in the cities in which they work and live.

Faced with such circumstances, low-wage, migrant workers are courageously organizing to defend their rights, to build power, and fight for dignity and respect. As workplace violations in low-wage industries put pressure on firms higher up the wage ladder to follow suit, these worker-organizers are leading a struggle to improve wages and conditions for all workers, their families, and their communities. At organizations such as Brandworkers and Retail Action Project in New York, or at Migrant Workers Home in Beijing, workers plan and execute their own campaigns, organizing to improve workplace conditions, and to help build a social justice movement. In this process, people who have been dispossessed of their land and livelihood, and who are often some of the most vulnerable and disenfranchised members of society, participate as active protagonists of social change. As low-wage, migrant workers persevere through determined struggle to win justice and respect, they are also claiming and enacting the right to citizenship, a right from which many have officially or unofficially been excluded.

The series of events at Ludlow 38 brought these issues to an art audience, while also looking at the ways in which people in the arts have supported worker-organizing campaigns, and at organizing that is happening in the arts. As class divisions within the art and culture industries become ever more pronounced, contract and temporary workers in these industries participate in the vast and varied informal economies that continue to expand at the centers of the world's metropolises. Finally, as the events at Ludlow 38 addressed issues that are relevant to audiences that extend beyond the boundaries of the art world, many who attended these events included workers, organizers, activists, students, scholars, as well as artists and art audiences.

A shopfront on 15 Bowery (Confucius Plaza), 2011
(Photo: Tobi Maier)

Confucius Plaza in Chinatown, New York, 2006
(Photo: Wally Gobetz)

CONFUCIANOMICS

By Amran Frey

During the Cultural Revolution Mao condemned Confucian thought and its followers as feudal and anti-revolutionary. The rejection of Confucianism as the exploitive classes' ideology led to an unprecedented suppression of the venerable lore, which served as China's ideological backbone from the second century AD until the Revolution of 1911 that brought an end to the late Qing Dynasty. In schools, children were taught to damn Confucius, as their parents were forced to chant curses on him at public demonstrations. A popular comic strip displayed a grinning philosopher next to a massacre of slaves. Red Guards were encouraged to demolish Confucian temples, bodies of his descendants were exhumed, and his ancestral home in Chu Fu, the village he was born in 2500 years ago, was destroyed. In 1974, a Chinese broadcast announced: "Although Confucius is dead, his corpse continues to emit its stench even today. Its poison is deep and its influence extensive." Yet in 1995, leaders of the Chinese Communist Party officially celebrated Confucius' 2545th birthday, bringing the decades old ban to an end. Since, Confucian rhetoric has been used with increasing regularity, and the building of a harmonious society has become a major objective in the Party's 21st century initiatives.

But what does the revival of this moral code mean for China's workers, the very people who were supposedly elevated through its demise? Alongside Confucianism's official come back, the Chinese economy has grown into a veritable powerhouse through the use of cheap labor that has been largely excluded from the country's new wealth. It is arguable that the selective promotion of Confucian thought has perpetuated social inequality, and served as a handy ideological tool for the Communist Party. And while the enforcement of workers' rights is unlikely to be achieved through a complete adoption of Western legal values, it needs to be argued for, with respect to Confucian legal tradition.

Tied to the pursuit of harmony through selflessness, Confucian governance relies the exaltation of a sage leader. The ruled owe loyalty and service to their rulers, while the rulers are obliged to provide for the welfare of their people. A leader is not controlled by political institutions, but by his moral commitment to his people. The degree of humanity and benevolence a leader displays is thus crucial, as it creates a standard for his subordinates. In the Analects, a major Confucian record written by the philosopher's students, we can find the following dialogue: "The Master said: When a Prince's personal conduct is correct, his government is effective without the issuing of orders. If his personal conduct is not correct, he may issue orders, but they will not be followed."

Yet when carefully selected, Confucian principles provide extensive ideological possibilities to serve all kinds of political motives. And as observers have commented, the revitalization proceeded so quickly that it resembles a Mao-era campaign. Read in this light, the deep rootedness of Confucianism in Chinese culture is not likely to be the catalyst behind this development. Rather, it seems that the Communist Party has fashioned itself into an unchallengeable and caring leader of "correct conduct" by selectively using Confucian teachings as a support pillar for the Party's authoritarian and paternalistic politics.

Facing widespread public skepticism of traditional Communist ideology, the Party needed to adopt a popular philosophy that would not overtly contradict existing Marxist policies, while coping with the ideological dilemmas wrought by market liberalization. Somehow the economic deregulations since the 1980's had to echo a familiar agenda. Although Confucian texts feature a strong disdain for profit, the carefully mediated revival of Confucianism has been used to deconstruct the anti-capitalist revolutionary ethos and replace it with an indigenous system that places Chinese culture within the narrative of global capitalism, and counters Western influences of rampant individualism.

Simultaneously, the Party has been able to obfuscate responsibility for social unrest, caused by poverty, income inequality, and poor working conditions by promoting Confucianism's vertical social hierarchy, and emphasis on self-constraint for the greater good of social harmony. However, to address Confucianism solely as a manipulated ideological tool does not give due credit to its role in Chinese political culture. We have to consider China's distinctive philosophical tradition, in total, when trying to understand how the Chinese people and their government are engaging 21st century challenges.

Today, the question, under what conditions the low-wage labor, that enabled China's rapid economic growth, will take place and how new wealth will be distributed is crucial to the country's future. The underpayment and non-payment of workers is a prevalent problem, and still calls for a sustainable solution. Non-payment occurs most often among migrant workers from the countryside, when they return to their villages in January to celebrate the Lunar New Year. Despite frequent calls for state intervention, and for the official criminalization of this conduct, the Chinese government has taken no serious action. Legal scholars Will Shen and Rohan Price argue that the alleged "lawlessness" has to be regarded and evaluated in the light of Confucian legal tradition.

Conceptually, early Confucianism subordinates law to morality, in a way that is not comparable to Western approaches. Unlike in other major civilizations, written law in early China was greeted with hostility as early Confucian thinkers equated codified law with moral decline, and at times even considered it a disturbance of the entire cosmic order. It was taught that a set of moral values should be impressed upon people by employing persuasion and example, while written law should be regarded as a last resort used to reinforce these moral standards.

A virtuous relationship partner, employee, subordinate or child appreciates his role, and will therefore defer his personal interests for the greater good of overall harmony in case of a conflict. The crucial virtue is gradually internalized as one becomes worthy of virtuous peoples' association, as good people reflect virtue onto each other. This way, people become humane individuals with a proper sense of shame, and are able to settle disputes through non-litigious means.

Taking issue with the view of Mencius and other disciples of Confucius that human nature was essentially good, *Southern Metropolis Daily* columnist Su Dahe commented earlier this year:

"It should be clear by now that unless the law is perfected in this regard, and the system really gets into gear, if I were the boss, I would withhold wages, too. Working for money is, I admit, an undeniable right, but it is my money you are working for. Do you think I will give you my money without a fight? If you curse me for not having a conscience, I will not deny it, and what's more, I will not care."

In the Confucian view, a boss without conscience is not virtuous, but that allegation does not solve the problem of unpaid workers. Regarding the worker, Confucianism would suggest that the he also lacks virtue, because otherwise he would have found employment under a virtuous boss who values harmony and fulfills his duties towards him.

To Western ears the described Confucian inference might sound cynical, however, in a 2003 survey conducted by sociologists Fenyu Wang and Yandong Zhao, many unfortunate members of the Chinese working class were found to blame their own insufficiency. Only five percent of polled workers laid-off by economic liberalization practices claimed that their minimal education and lack of skills made it too difficult to find new employment, and viewed their situation as a problem that stems from them. In contrast, surveys of unemployed Germans state mostly external reasons like companies' greedy policies or increased industrial mechanization, not their lack of virtue. Chinese workers' notions of virtue and dignity include a distinct assumption of self-responsibility, and may have delayed the outbreak of strikes and protests. But no tradition can ultimately exempt the government from dealing with the social consequences of China's economic development.

To restore harmony between companies and the workforce, a Confucian leader would have to establish moral authority as a role model employer. However, it is highly questionable whether it would affect abusive policies of a private corporation, if its management came to know that the state-run competitor next door voluntarily abides labor law and labor contracts. As is, employees' rights, that were supposed to be established by China's extensive labor law legislation, often remain mere theory, waiting for either a virtuous employer or for the alarmingly low rate of executed judgments to shift. Corruption, and the official protection of larger businesses can be identified as reasons for the circumstances, but assuming that the prevalence of profit maximization is the only cause might not do justice to the issue's complexity.

Unlike in most Western countries, the judiciary is constitutionally weakened and can hardly establish rule of law, while the administrative authority is better equipped and more influential than the courts. Therefore courts are often not in the position to be proactive in the implementation of labor standards. The underlying understanding of government corresponds to the Confucian aim of limiting the usage of law, which also manifests itself in contemporary Chinese business life. Here, mutual trust and harmonious long-term relationships are strongly preferred to an enforceable civil judgment that would endanger the former. This cultural imprint is furthermore reflected in recent labor legislation, such as the Labor Dispute Mediation and Arbitration Law, which came into effect in May 2008.

This legislation provides a comprehensive framework for the mediation process in labor disputes and vigorously encourages mediation as the favored approach for resolution. As Article 1 states the promotion of harmonious and stable relations, parties are urged to take several non-litigious steps before being able to take legal action in front of the People's Court. Consultation is followed by mediation within a corporate committee in which both employees and employers are equally represented. If no settlement is achieved, the parties have to apply to the local labor dispute arbitration commission. In most cases it is only after these steps that one can go to court. This law exemplifies the elaborate legal infrastructure, however, none of it is not worth much if it does not enable workers to ultimately enforce their rights.

Current social tensions in China suggest that, eventually, the discrepancies between the large body of labor legislation and the enforcement practice will have to be counteracted. A series of recent high profile strikes and suicide cases anticipate a turning point in China's development. Since the 1980s, increases in workers' wages have not corresponded to the overall economic growth, which was based on the seemingly endless availability of cheap labor. Due to the extensive potential workforce and extreme poverty in China's vast economic hinterlands, many companies used to get away with providing mere subsistence for their workers. But today, family planning policies, increased job opportunities in rural areas, and a new generation of migrant workers have led to labor shortages.

In the eastern province of Jiangsu, more than sixty percent of businesses expect to face hiring problems according to a survey published in February 2011. Companies encounter a generation of better educated and Internet savvy workers that have higher expectations than their parents and grandparents. Being increasingly aware of their legal rights and leverage within Chinese economy, many of them are demanding a higher standard of living that allows for more pleasure and self-fulfillment. After the strikes and protests of 2010 halted the production at many key foreign firms, companies were forced to react, and many agreed to pay rises between twenty and one hundred percent of existing monthly salaries. In a situation in which workers are more and more in the position to endanger China's economic stability, the government will have to take their demands seriously and cannot rely on Confucian rhetoric or other ideological strongholds in place of effective provisions.

While providing for workers' minimum needs may meet Confucian requirements for leadership, the Chinese government will have to find a more balanced approach to secure stable relationships between businesses and their employees. From a Western perspective, the establishment of effective legal institutions and rule of law seems imperative to achieve this goal.

However, further diffusion of political power and the recognition of individual rights will not develop as something that completely displaces traditional Chinese approaches to solving economic and social disputes. The way the relationship between harmony and law is regarded in Chinese culture, and the powerful position of the administrative authority will inevitably frame China's way to a more just system.

Workers may hope, that the influence of Confucian values will allow for a system that accommodates both the Chinese preference for non-litigious dispute, and stronger legal institutions better equipped to enforce labor regulations.

The following essays are based on lectures held at the symposium

PRECARIOUS POWER: SYNDICALISM, SOLIDARITY, AND THE NEW ORGANIZATIONAL PARADIGM, on July 16, 2011 at Murphy Institute for Worker Education and Labor Studies, CUNY, New York City.

S Y M P O S I U M

INTRODUCTION

By Immanuel Ness

This is an exceptionally propitious time to examine the steep secular decline of working class power, the hollowing out of trade unions, and the widespread expansion of precarious labor. In an environment of eroding union power, the possibility of new forms of labor organization is on the horizon as workers will always resist employer domination. I define precarious labor as the new constellation of workers employed in temporary and contingent jobs who are paid extremely low wages, do not have access to health care, are more and more vulnerable to social isolation and employer repression.

In the second decade of the 21st century, workers deemed "precarious" now comprise a majority of the labor force in the global North and South and are found disproportionately among migrant laborers. In the US, as traditional labor unions that were formed primarily by immigrant workers in the early-20th century have absolutely failed to represent most contingent workers, we are witnessing the steady growth in the autonomous resistance outside of traditional trade union organizations. This newfound resistance is found increasingly through self-organizing by autonomous workers in what I call "parallel unions" formed by workers on the job and within oppressed communities overlooked by the mainstream organized labor organizations. While precarious labor organization is unauthorized by state laws, lack of institutional arrangements, and the national status of workers, precarious laborers without established union representation are using new means to advance their interest. Precarious workers may exert their power to improve immediate workplace conditions by engaging slowdowns, strikes, and enterprise occupations. Unlike traditional unions, precarious workers make immediate demands that reflect a syndicalist working-class culture of workers who band together to defend a common set of interests. While most workers are prevented from striking through bargaining arrangements, precarious workers without equivalent rights ironically have more power to walk off the job or occupy factories as no government institutions are in place to referee labor-management relations in workplaces that are not administered by labor law regimes. I define syndicalism in the present era as militant actions by workers in new forms of labor organizations that reject the status quo of capitalist hegemony in the workplace and oppose traditional unions as intermediaries in their struggles with employers. As such, syndicalist unions reject the legitimacy of capitalist domination over society. Given the insecure and unpredictable nature of their work, precarious and migrant workers must demand immediate improvements of their wages and conditions rather than long-term contracts that may take months to approve—and agreements that are frequently rooted in concessions to capital rather than demands for higher wages and conditions through democratic participation. Syndicalists do not require trade union bureaucrats as intermediaries who pretend to represent their interests, but in reality, reduce worker militancy. More than any time since the 1940s, workers in the 2010s recognize that their power lies in their capacity to withhold their labor and disrupt typically miserable workplace conditions.

I will briefly discuss the significance of what we are witnessing at this historical context before we hear from our distinguished speakers.

The revitalization of syndicalism and autonomism as meaningful working-class organizing practice is a clear challenge to established bureaucratic unions, parties, and governing institutions that have long accepted the dominance of capital over the state and society. Over the past two generations the New Deal labor-capital class compromises of the 1930s have been abrogated by business, severely grinding down worker power. After 75 years of labor concessions, government cutbacks, and inimical legal decisions, workers' memory of successful past struggles have been fully extinguished. No matter, workers retain a sense of indignation over exploitation and an aspiration for democratic control over the conditions of their work and communities. Why should we be so surprised if businesses continue to reduce wages and working conditions of workers? I think we can always expect employers to conduct themselves tyrannically against the working-class, lacking empathy for their victims who they exploit and torment over and again. However, what is surprising is that labor unions have not resisted through democratically mobilizing their members. Workers today increasingly recognize that the state is rooted in capitalist domination and that the very basis of the system must be challenged in the workplace rather than through amorphous demonstrations, which do not directly confront capital. Thus the real struggles must take place directly against capitalist enterprises and state institutions that defend their interests. While demonstrating against unjust laws discredits the state, strikes and direct action in workplaces challenge capital. Traditional unions who are unwilling to mobilize their members to strike are thus sustaining capitalist exploitation. No wonder workers are increasingly distrustful of them. But the historic record demonstrates an unbroken record of working class resistance against capital.

Even as trade unions and worker organizations have declined from the 1970s to the present, capital has accumulated almost unqualified power over workers, whether union members or not. Capital's insatiable and successful search for profits that has led to a new capitalist offensive against the working class, delegitimizing hierarchical unions and creating the opportunity for new forms of working class organization through worker self organization. Even in China, workers are succeeding in improving their conditions through shop-floor committees that place demands on the state-dominated All-China Federation of Trade Unions for better wages, housing, and health care. As more workers throughout the world lack democratic representation, or are excluded from participation in traditional unions, similar resistance is escalating among precarious workers in the global North and South. Both transnational and internal migrant workers who form bonds of solidarity in their communities are particularly apt at challenging the system.

Neoliberal economic restructuring, destabilization of unionized labor markets that once provided living wages, coupled with the financialization of the economy, is undermining the capacity of global, regional, and national plans for expanding capitalist neoliberalism. Now, nearly 3 years after the economic shocks of 2008, workers and the poor in communities in the US and throughout the world are suffering the consequences of yet a new round of reductions of social and public services to pacify financial markets that are unable and unwilling to produce economic stability.

Serious capital market analysts always recognized that the working class and the poor suffer from government retrenchment. But in past recessions, few worried about the fate of precarious workers. Let me quote from a recent article that appeared on June 27, 2011, in *The Financial Times*, which, along with the *Wall Street Journal,* is the principal daily source of news source for the investment capitalists:

As a result of stagnant wages and poverty in the advanced capitalist world, we are observing a "specter of stagnating incomes" from North America, to Europe, and the Far East. Workers in no country are immune to this trend. Even Germany's economic stability is accompanied by declining wages. The British capitalist newspaper of record even contends that the "financial sector, found ways to make fortunes gambling with other people's money."

Just as labor unions have failed their members, the political and electoral system of the state is also failing the majority.

Industrial Workers of the World, 2005

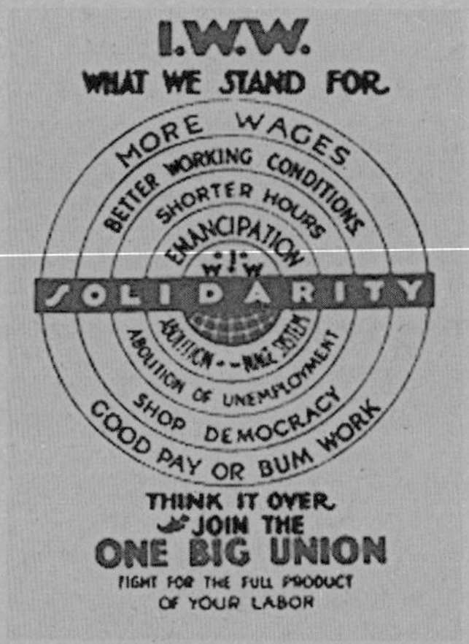

Industrial Workers of the World, 2011

We must recognize that popular working-class forces can no longer just elect liberal or democratic governments and expect Keynesian labor-friendly policies. For 20 years since the fall of the Soviet Union, liberal and social democratic parties, almost to a fault—have welcomed the same neoliberal formula that erodes living standards through degrading labor standards. Equally, traditional unions, which have served as intermediaries between capital and labor can no longer justify themselves when they are unable to even ensure a living wage and are permitting greater numbers of workers to fall into precarious living conditions. They merely become a drag on labor. Given that traditional unions have engaged in patterns of concessions since the 1970s, there is very little left to give up, and their leaders and vertical structures are ignored by corporations and increasingly curbing the potential ideological power of working people.

Thus we must reject the autocratic and increasingly tyrannical rule of state authorities that are expressing the will of corporations and rely on the self-organizing capacities of workers. The state, unions and capital have failed in all their policies over the last forty or fifty years whether Keynesianism or under contemporary Neoliberalism, which is stripping away all forms of social protection for the working class through eliminating social welfare in a system where legal structures from past generations prevent working class mobilization and strikes. Neoliberal capitalism has worn away all the defenses that workers struggled for in the mid-20th century while maintaining the legal restraints against labor militancy through abolishing workers of their most effective weapons of resistance: withholding their labor power, occupying factories, offices, and banks, and disrupting the everyday flow of business. Due to the readiness of the state to use mass incarceration and violence, organized labor, accustomed to stable contracts and bargaining relationships are under extreme pressure to surrender. Thus I assert that new syndicalist and autonomist collective action rooted in the centrality of the working will become the most effective strategy that workers can embark upon. .... whether they are forcing their traditional unions to resist the further erosion of their living standards or autonomously challenging capitalist prerogatives in these "parallel unions" that may or may not have officially recognized names and local numbers, but are rooted in the self-organization of the working class.

Due to the tremendous toll and denial of rights, the historic capitalist compromises of the 1930s that gained union recognition and collective bargaining are threatened on a daily basis. But were these compromises really an expression of the aspirations and hopes of workers? Absolutely not! A century ago, workers considered union membership in syndicalist and militant organization a form of power that could lead to democratic transformation of workplaces. Yet they were stymied and over the course of the past 75 years cynically recognize the powerlessness inherent in traditional union structures and bargaining with an enemy intent on their destruction as forces of resistance.

As labor historian David Brody argues, we can expect the capitalist class to act like the beasts of the field. While many workers felt that union membership would translate into social revolution, few imagined that labor unions would serve as the handmaiden of the capitalist class through restraining their own member's militancy. The Industrial Workers of the World rejected the notion of bargaining with a state that is bound to advancing capitalist interests and were correct in founding unions rooted in democratic and solidaristic practice. As a consequence, today, workers recognize that unions will neither protect their economic well-being nor lead the path to democratizing workplaces.

As a result, workers are implicitly contemplating new forms of struggle and worker representation that rejects bureaucracy and the simplistic notion that liberal-bourgeois parliamentary states are capable of transforming themselves. The Great Recession demonstrates the futility of both Keynesianism and free market solutions as an antidote for advancing worker rights. As more people are pushed into precarious jobs or into unemployment, we must learn from global examples from Argentina, Brazil, the Arab world, and throughout Europe.

As István Metsaros avers, we must not be trapped in the misconception that parliamentary systems are democratic. Even conservative scholars like Joseph Schumpeter argued that the working class is no threat as long as they are duped into believing that they actually have democratic rights beyond voting every few years for political party representatives that share a vision in advancing corporate profits at the expense of workers.

I envision a society evolving with precarious and immigrant worker organizations co-existing with traditional unions. Thus, IWW syndicalists, autonomists, and council communists are likely to coexist at least in the near term, with the traditional unions who are mostly ineffective in representing the working class, no less than their own members. Workers and unions must resist class collaborationist unionism that is the basis upon which countries in advanced societies operate by buying of unions. In the last 15 years, in every continent and country, workers' self-activity is propagating new forms of union organization that oppose government and capitalist sponsored unions. Just to mention a few examples: in Argentina, new unions are forming to challenge ossified teachers and food processing unions.

It is particularly important to recognize the monumental efforts of Greek and Spanish workers challenging government and IMF efforts to erode wages and working conditions. Indeed the Arab spring is rooted in neoliberal efforts to undermine working conditions.

We must understand these movements of workers rooted in concrete struggles rather than abstractions. Each struggle by workers in factories, mines, hospitals, and retail establishments are crucial in determining the direction of the struggle. But we must remember worker insurrections are not abstractions, but reflect authentic demands and expectations of workers who must recognize that they can gain power as collectivities who determine their own fate, rather than as tools of labor organizers. In the United States and here in New York City, we must identify these struggles and form alliances with workers who are resisting public and private employers. Given bureaucracy and hierarchical organization inflects both capitalist enterprises and traditional unions. The new autonomist and syndicalist workers movements will determine the trajectory of the struggle for socialism and workers democracy.

CHINESE MIGRANT LABOR AND THE GLOBAL ECONOMY

By Jeff Becker

While the domestic US press is more likely to discuss China's impact on the world economy, the international economy has had a profound impact on China as well. This chapter discusses China's international economic integration and its impact on the nation's labor market, particularly China's domestic migrant labor population.

Chinese migrant workers (*nongmingong*) are peasant farmers who travel to urban areas in search of work, and are a critical component of the Chinese labor force. 2011 government figures estimate the total number of migrant workers to be over 240 million, with interprovincial migration alone topping 150 million.[1] Migrant workers in China constitute roughly 20–30% of the labor force, and the majority of the workforce in the nation's construction and manufacturing industries. Moreover, as recent labor unrest in companies such as Honda and the Apple supplier Foxconn have demonstrated, China's new generation of migrants are increasingly assertive in pursuing their rights.

China's Entry into International Markets: The Creation of Migrant Labor

China's entry into the international trade system had a direct hand in the creation of migrant labor as a distinct component of the work force. The dismantling of the rural commune system, a holdover from the state run command economy, freed up vast amounts of rural labor. Increased attention to light industry and manufacturing provided incentives for farmers to move to the cities. Simultaneously, the government began downgrading many of the rudimentary social and health services available in the countryside, creating both incentives to migrate and disincentives to stay. Government policies directed the flow of this migration as well; into the southern Pearl River Delta for example, where new Special Economic Zones (SEZs) focused on producing goods for export.

Throughout these early years of economic reform, migrant workers occupied a very precarious position in society. Despite working in the cities, they were not considered true urban citizens. Like all citizens, migrant workers were, and still are, subject to the household (*hukou*) registration system, which ties access to social services to one's place of birth. Thus, because they were born in the countryside, migrant workers did not receive the same social benefits as their urban counterparts, and were restricted in their ability to access education, housing, and other social protections. Migrants were also subject to routine harassment from the state and criminal elements.

Despite these difficulties however, China's migrant population continued to grow. In the early 1980s, some estimates put the number of "mobile migrants" at approximately 2 million workers. By 1989 the same measure put the number of migrants at roughly 30 million.[2]

Complexities in the Chinese Labor Market: Opportunities for Exploitation

As the Chinese economy evolved throughout the 1990s and into the 2000s, mass quantities of cheap migrant labor helped make China the "workshop of the world." Yet this dramatic transition to export led development also created ample opportunities for labor exploitation. At one level, government and party officials focusing solely on economic growth contributed to an environment where government and business worked hand in hand, often at the expense of workers. In addition however, China's state regulatory institutions simply had trouble keeping up with rapid changes in the labor market.

Two types of labor relationships, those involving the use of labor contractors (*baogongtou*) and labor dispatch services (*paiqian gongsi*) provide an excellent example of this challenge. Labor contractors, individuals acting as a third party between workers and the entity receiving the work, became common at this time, particularly in industries requiring large amounts of short-term or temporary labor such as construction. Limited protections for workers against contractors however, and little if any formal relationship between migrant workers and the companies for whom they were actually doing the work, meant that migrants employed by contractors were ripe for exploitation. For example, companies often paid wages directly to the contractor, and should the contractor fail to receive payment from the parent company or decide to abscond with workers' wages, workers were left in a difficult position, having no formal relationship with the construction company to help them prove the "factual labor relationship" necessary to attain legal redress.

Labor dispatch services, companies that provide employers with large amounts of short term labor, provide another example of rapid changes in the labor market creating opportunities for exploitation. As labor dispatch services began appearing in the Chinese economy, laws governing this tripartite relationship between the service, the worker, and the company receiving the work, remained largely undefined. Legal and regulatory confusion allowed both the labor dispatch company and the employer to claim that workers' salary and benefits were responsibility of the other party. Because Chinese legal institutions lacked the tools to manage these relationships, decisions regarding responsibility often stalled, and often at workers' expense.

Labor's Response to Exploitation: Tiaolou and Manhunts

Ironically, it was not until the situation began to improve that China witnessed a substantial rise in migrant labor protests. To be sure, motivation was never an issue, yet in the 1980s and 1990s, migrant workers were more severely restricted when operating in urban areas, and often lacked the social space necessary to engage in the types of collective actions seen today.

Since the mid-2000s however, the situation of China's migrants has gradually improved. Legislation such as the *Labor Contract Law* (2008) and the *Labor Dispute*

1 National Bureau of Statistics, *Statistical Communiqué of the People's Republic of China on the 2010 National Economic and Social Development*, 2 Februar, 2011, http://www.stats.gov.cn/was40/gjtjj_en_detail.jsp?searchword=migrant+workers&channelid=9528&record=1.

2 *Peasant Migrants Creates Both Opportunity and Challenges for Society*, [Nongmingong Liudong wei Shehui Fazhan Dailai Jiyu yu Tiaozhan,] *Peasant Daily*, 16 September, 2008, available at http://www.agri.gov.cn/llzy/t20080916_1133319.htm.

Tiaolou as a form of migrant labor protest in China

Mediation and Arbitration Law (2008) provided additional protections for all of China's workers, including migrants. Migrant workers are also now considered members of the working class, and are heavily recruited by the All-China Federation of Trade Unions. While biases against migrants in the city remain, they are considered legitimate, if still second-class, members of urban society. In addition, China's younger generation of migrants are more educated, more conscious of their rights under the law, and more comfortable operating in the cities. Indeed, many of China's new generation of migrants consider themselves to be "new urban citizens" (*xin shimin*), and have no intention of following their predecessors back to the countryside.

Given migrant workers' expanded space and increased self-confidence in urban environments, how have they protested their unfair treatment? Use of the formal legal system, including labor arbitration and courts, is one commonly used option, as are traditional strikes, traffic disruptions, and other forms of collective protests. This final section however briefly describes two lesser-discussed forms of protest activity; manhunts and *tiaolou*.

Simply stated, manhunts are an attempt by a group of workers to locate their employer in order to retrieve back pay. Despite laws prohibiting companies from paying wages directly to labor contractors as described above, the practice persists. When this happens, one option workers have is to try resolving the dispute by confronting their labor contractor directly. This is one reason why migrant workers in construction often express a preference for working with a contractor from their hometown. Not only are they more likely to have developed a sense of trust with the individual, but they have a better chance of finding him should he fail to pay wages. One individual I interviewed during the course of my research for example was from Hebei, working on a construction site in Beijing with about 30 other workers. When they discovered that their contractor had left town without paying the last of their wages, the group traveled in mass to this individual's home, threatening the contractor's wife unless they received their wages.

Another unorthodox yet increasingly common strategy for protest is *tiaolou*, a tactic that involves climbing buildings, bridges, or unfinished scaffolding, and threatening to jump. Starting in the early 2000s, China witnessed a sharp rise in the number of *tiaolou* protests reported in the mainland press. By the late 2000s, *tiaolou* had become a common occurrence in regions with large migrant populations. The Guangzhou government for example estimated at least one *tiaolou* event occurred every 4 days on Haizhu Bridge, an important transportation thoroughfare in Guangzhou city. The government also estimated that one 5 hour *tiaolou* event at Haizhu Bridge cost approximately 1 million RMB (about $158,000) in transportation and shipping delays.[3]

Conclusion:
China's Migrants in the Global Economy

China's entrance into the global economy had a dramatic impact on its labor market, helping to create a new segment of the labor force. Policies of reform and opening in the early 1980s required greater labor flexibility, and as surplus labor travelled to emerging boom towns in the Pearl and Yangtze River Delta, this created a new type of worker that did not fit the traditional "peasant-worker" dichotomy. As China's economy became more closely integrated with the rest of the world, new labor relationships such as labor dispatch emerged, while some relationships not seen for decades, such as labor contractors, reappeared. These relationships provided flexibility in the labor market necessary for China to act as the "workshop of the world," yet these changes did little to protect the nation's labor force.

As political, social, and economic changes began to provide migrants with additional space to operate in the cities, their "repertoires of contention" began to expand. Migrants protested their exploitation using the developing legal system, traditional collective actions, and more unorthodox protests such as those described above. As the Chinese government continues to manage the aftermath of the global economic recession, China's economic policy decision will no doubt have continued consequences for the future evolution of its emerging migrant labor class.

3 Qiu Feng, *Why Do We Have Sympathy for Tiaolou?* [Women Weisha Tongqing Tiaolouzhi], *China Newsweek*, 2009, no. 20.

Creative Communication *Project Retailing* in New York City by Retail Action Project, 2011

Subversive Coupons by Retail Action Project, 2010

SYMPOSIUM

PRECARITY ON THE RETAIL FRONTLINES

By Carrie Gleason

The growth of service industry employment coupled with diminished living wage job opportunities means that more families than ever are now relying on retail work. The retail sector has been one of the fastest growing U.S. industries, employing over 14 million people (U.S. Bureau of Labor Statistics 2010), and its growth continues despite the current economic downturn. However, across industry tiers—from mass-market chains to high-end department stores—retailers are shifting towards just-in-time workforce hiring more part-time workers with less predictable schedules. As the industry expands, more and more American retail workers are seeing their earning potential eroded, involuntarily working fewer hours and juggling two part-time jobs with shifting schedules. The struggle for the 40-hour workweek has come full circle for American service industry workers—now the fight is get enough hours to get by.

Retail and much of the service economy has seasonal periods of high and low employment. Historically retailers have had a core of full-time workers and hired additional temporary help during seasonal highs. However, among some retailers, part-time workers now dominate their workforce, with full-time positions relegated only to management. 41 percent of frontline retail workers are employed part-time; and those part-time workers earn about 33 percent less than do full-time retail workers (Tilly, Carré and Appelbaum, 2008). Part-time workers cost less because companies save on unemployment insurance connected to lay-offs, reduced benefit eligibility and higher turnover that keeps wages low. Thus, we have seen the part-time workforce grow from 5.3 million in 2008 to 8.6 million involuntary part-time workers in 2010 (U.S. Bureau of Labor Statistics June 2008, 2010).

Since hourly workers' eligibility for health benefits and paid time off is linked to the amount of hours worked, scheduling is a way to diminish the number of workers eligible for costly benefits. Only 16.4 percent of part-time retail workers have employer-based health coverage (Lambert 2008: 1206; CPS 2006). Typically employers have policies stating a minimum number of hours required for benefits eligibility. Full-time hours, usually 30-35 hours per week, is becoming the industry standard for benefits eligibility. Manhattan *Adidas* workers reported in January 2011 the company stopped offering health insurance to part-time workers. Indeed, where companies offer health benefits to part-time workers, managers have been known to purposely schedule workers for less than the hours needed to meet benefits eligibility. At a growing number of stores, including *Tommy Hilfiger, Muji* and *Crocs,* managers are the only full-time workers and thus are the only workers eligible for health benefits. *Uniqlo* and *JC Penney* workers have reported losing their benefits when they worked reduced hours as a consequence of an illness.

Store managers experience intense pressure to keep labor costs down. Pressures to stay within schedule budgets have led to labor law violations in some companies. Assistant managers at *Foot Locker* won class action certification for their 2007 lawsuit alleging that store managers altered workers' timesheets in order to avoid overtime pay. In the plaintiffs' legal complaint, assistant managers alleged that store managers violated state and federal labor laws "to meet budgetary constraints concerning total payroll per store," and because "managers get penalized if they exceed those budgets." Labor law violations for failure to pay minimum wage and overtime are prevalent in the retail industry. However, the *Foot Locker* case is remarkable because it involves systemic violations at a national corporate retailer.

Managers use the scheduling of workers' hours for discipline and rewards. Thus retail workers have incredibly flexible, yet rigid schedules. While companies have the power to change hours without notice, workers are often penalized for any unplanned absence such as a sick day (Henly et al. 2006: 623). Lambert's study highlights how "structured instability" is a common labor management practice in the retail industry (Lambert 2008: 1220). It's not just about part-time work—retail workers across the industry are finding their start and end-times, shifts and number of hours vary weekly often with minimal advanced notice (Henly, Shaefer and Waxman 2006: 619; Lambert 2008: 1207). Unplanned hour reductions are prevalent and extra hours one day usually means fewer hours the next day, and call-in shifts are on the rise. Workers from *Radioshack* to *Victoria's Secret* report that the corporate office will—with no advance notice—reduce scheduled hours if customer traffic or purchases are lower than predicted. Managers often do not notify workers of their scheduling changes, even if the changes are made just a few hours before the employee is scheduled. A Connecticut *Radioshack* worker had this to say about her scheduling issues:

> "Last week I arrived at 10am, but my manager told me I was an hour early because my schedule was changed to 11am. The next day I arrived at 10am and she told me not to clock in because I was an hour late. I didn't know my schedule had been changed to 9am. She told me not to bother to come in the rest of the week."

The notion of "structured instability" as a labor management practice spotlights how corporations are not just skimming hours, but rather are actively encouraging employment instability in the retail workforce. From *American Eagle Outfitter* to *Henri Bendel* front line retail workers are getting as few as 8-15 hours a week. Hours have become the new bonus in retail. Larger retailers are now using computerized scheduling software that schedules workers' hours (how much and when workers work) according to projected sales—increasingly in real time, thanks to innovations from *Walmart* (Lambert 2008: 1224). As Susan Lambert argues, frontline retail workers are increasingly paying the price of market fluctuations. For retail workers living paycheck to paycheck, the difference of a few hours of work can mean getting by or falling behind. Hours fluctuate and workers face eviction notices, mounting credit card debt, hungry days and phone-lines cut off. This is the reality of far too many workers in one of America's top growth industries. It's time we expect more of the retailers that are creating jobs and putting America back to work.

Through scheduling and excessive employee-sanctions, retailers' labor management practices are sometimes designed to encourage turnover. Turnover helps to manage the size of the workforce and is factored into manager's budgeting of hours in their weekly schedules (Lambert 2008: 1219). It also lessens workers' claims on the company for raises, better conditions and unionization. Workers are "set-up" to quit through scheduling practices such as undesirable shifts, erratic start and end-times, too

Demonstration against wage theft in New York City by Retail Action Project, 2011

few hours and excessive discipline for minor infractions. This leads workers to quit out of frustration or just stop showing up for work. For many of these workers, quitting feels more dignified than continuing to show up to work to face disrespectful management. Yet, workers who quit or abandon the job are typically ineligible for unemployment.

Who is most affected by this new burden? People of color —especially African Americans—women, immigrants and those with less formal education have been hit hardest. In New York City where three in five retail workers earn low-wages, nearly 70 percent of the retail workforce is composed of people of color and half are immigrants (Parrott et al. 2008). Women are 64 percent of the part-time front line retail workers, yet women hold only 33 percent of the management positions. *Walmart* recently battled what would have been one of the largest gender discrimination lawsuits in history—with barriers to promotions, pay inequity and sexual harassment as chief complaints of the 1.6 million plaintiffs were denied justice by the Supreme Court.

As retailers are now demanding complete flexibility from their employees, 'open availability' can be a requirement to get hired. This coupled with erratic scheduling practices make it difficult for workers to get second jobs or go to school. Thus lowering their potential for personal income growth. These practices also pose serious challenges to families—including childcare, homework support, sleeping schedules, and doctor's appointments (Henly, Shaefer and Waxman 2006). In short, employer-driven non-standard work schedules hurt low-income families.

A 2010 White House report on the economics of workplace flexibility acknowledged that professional workers have more 'workplace flexibility' while less-skilled workers have significantly less flexibility in their work. For professional workers, workplace flexibility means they are able to adjust their hours to meet family and personal commitments. For low-wage workers, particularly in the service industry, "flexibility means erratic schedules, stress, less control over your work life and scrambling to meet the needs of your family" (Lambert 2008). The continuum from a 'flexible workforce' to 'workplace flexibility' is delineated by how much power workers have in the setting of their hours.

The shift towards a part-time workforce is justified by a de-valuing of the skills demanded by fast paced customer service work required in most frontline retail jobs. Retail is not a low-skilled job. Retail workers advise customers, accessorize to sell goods, handle customer after customer with a smile, operate cash registers accurately and efficiently, catalog and transport merchandise, set up visual displays, order new shipments, reduce loss prevention, build client books and the list goes on. A strategy to improve retail jobs must include an effort to re-value the labor it takes to sell the merchandise that generates retailers' profits.

The retail industry has a growing role to play in our economic recovery as one of the few industries offering jobs. Thus we need to raise the public's expectations for the quality of jobs the retail industry should provide. With its policy and research, organizing and media efforts, our growing organization of New York City retail workers, the *Retail Action Project,* seeks to build power to secure the hours, pay, and working conditions that retail workers, their families and communities need to thrive.

BIBLIOGRAPHY

Henly, Julia R., H. Luke Shaefer, and Elaine Waxman. 2006. *Nonstandard Work Schedules: Employer- and Employee-Driven Flexibility in Retail Jobs.* Social Service Review (December). Chicago, IL: The University of Chicago, pp.609–634.

J. Lambert, Susan. 2008. *Passing the buck: Labor flexibility practices that transfer risk onto hourly workers,* Human Relations 61; 1203.

Parrott, James, David Syssegaard Kallick, and Michele Mattingly. 2008. *Low Wages, No Bargain: Retail Jobs in New York City,* Fiscal Policy Institute, December.

Rogers, Joel. 1995. *A Strategy for Labor.* Industrial Relations, 34(3), July. Cambridge, MA: Blackwell Publishers.

Tilly, Chris. 2010. *Globalization? What Globalization? How National Institutions Determine Job Quality in Retail Around the World.* UCLA. Presentation of paper, New School for Social Research, February 25.

Tilly, Chris, Françoise Carré, and Lauren D. Appelbaum. 2010 *Competitive Strategies and Worker Outcomes in the US Retail Industry.* UCLA, Institute for Research on Labor and Employment, Research & Policy Brief, (5), June.

White House Council of Economic Advisors. 2010. *Work-Life Balance and the Economics of Workplace Flexibility.*

Installation *Tate Modern: Tomorrow Is Another Day (After the Economic Crisis)* produced by Not An Alternative for the Tate Modern's 10th anniversary show *No Soul for Sale: A Festival of Independents*. Not An Alternative, 2010

NOT AN ALTERNATIVE

By Beka Economopoulos

Not An Alternative is a hybrid arts collective and non-profit organization that focuses on the intersection of art, activism, technology, and theory. Based out of *No Space* in Williamsburg, Brooklyn, Not An Alternative curates programs and collaborates with other cultural producers and community organizations for artistic practices.

As so-called hipsters, we are a class that rejects any form of collective identity and does not acknowledge itself as a class. How do you organize a class that does not see itself as one and that is in fact defined by its disavowal? To answer this we have to look at how classes are defined now in contemporary societies. We would argue that there is a range of ways in which classes are defined. They are very obviously defined as a group of people who share common interests and perform common tasks. Classes are physically and geographically located in the same place. But we have to consider that now the economy is driven by a new form of extraction of wealth and appropriation of cultural capital. Liberal capitalism functions to subsume and to commodify and it is orientated around the logical participation. In the age of interactive media and industries that manufacture desires, we find ourselves increasingly manipulated in political and social situations. Participation is marked as a cultural imperative.

You are on *Facebook* whether you have a profile or not, somebody probably tagged you there. This is the age of interactivity, where participation is everything and nothing. Every action is subsumed by this new framework our likes and dislikes, our comments and curiosities, our mindless searches and our indiscriminate clicks; they are all analyzed and monetized by the new labor force.

Co-working is the model of the creative class. At No Space we work in different professions such as web development, design or journalism by side. We are geoflex and independent, we can work from anywhere. Thus, classes now are less defined by geography and physical specificity and more around proclivities and desires. The creation of classes in the daily adverts is really the engine for the creative industry workers such as the designer, the architects and the 3-D-animators. However, it is the question of gaining class awareness, which currently does not exist. This class awareness would lead to an understanding how the individual fits into the cycle of economical production and how it is related to it.

How can you understand your position transforming from one in which wealth is extracted from the work in your life to one in which you can use your position as a tool to express political agency? That is the question Not An Alternative is concerned with. The Brooklyn neighborhoods of Williamsburg and Greenpoint experienced New York City's most aggressive rezoning, with an estimated 10% population increase in less than a decade. Williamsburg and Greenpoint, an environmentally overburdened area, were processing 2/3 of New York City's trash along the waterfront. Many community groups were organizing around the issue and investigating ten years before the rezoning started. They collaborated with urban planners; they surveyed the community and developed a community plan for the rezoning in a participatory process as an alternative to the city's plan.

As a powerful gesture of activism, they organized a giant walkout of hundreds of people when the city was presenting its own plan for the rezoning, which looked absolutely nothing like the community plan. There were members of the Latin American and of the Polish community, but unfortunately, there were not a lot of hipsters. There isn't agency or power within that story. Ironically hipsters defend Brooklyn against nothing, and yet they are the protagonists in this story of gentrification. The hipsters find themselves in this endless displacement, being the agents of gentrification whether they like it or not.

Not An Alternative is interested in narratives that hipsters could understand and identify with, that could be potentially transformative and cast them in a different role. Referring to the movie *The Warriors* some people from the independent music and fashion scene in Williamsburg formed a group called *The Williamsburg Warriors*. Designing a concept envisioning what Williamsburg could be, the Warriors wanted to juxtapose the community plan with the city plan rather than the hipsters being dismissed. This was an image then that hipsters could identify with. Not An Alternative and The Williamsburg Warriors put the symbols of development in the community's hands like pick axes and shovels.

When we found out that the community was really fractured around very traditional thought lines we started using tactics that would mobilize the paralyzed community. Around this time Not An Alternative designed little buttons marked *We are no Soho,* thinking through these cultural touch points to engage people and create a new inclusive community. In addition Not An Alternative created a creative industry's coalition following Richard Florida, who is the love child of urban planners today. About a hundred local businesses signed on to this creative industry's coalition. Using this coalition as leverage the activists could fight back against gentrification and for the community plan with their symbols such as the shovel.

Ultimately the community adopted these symbols and also wore headbands from the Williamsburg Warriors to meetings, press conferences, marches and park reclamations. The community, including Latinos, seniors, hipsters etc., was united under this banner of the community plan with these symbols and tools of the community's self-determination, protesting against the city's top down decision with regards to the Williamsburg-Greenpoint rezoning. The city's presentation to sell their new rezoning proposal to the community was an idealized scenario with people of different ages and races. The plan looked like a projected fantasy for the people to step into, a utopic future the community should identify with. However, this computer simulation had nothing to do with the reality. In this variety of tactics, we have to keep in mind Richard Florida's concept of the creative class and his definition of this class that expedites. The identity of the creative class is one that we can use in leverage if we understand ourselves as a part of it, and not be so married necessarily to the identity of a counter culture, the subculture or the alternative form but rather to understand ourselves as an engine of culture and to step into that role. It has a responsibility that comes with it, to stand shoulder to shoulder with our fellow community members to fight back and continue to create and shape the future we seek.

<u>*THE HANNS EISLER NAIL SALON / NAIL WORKERS CHORUS*</u> *(H.E.N.S. / N.W.C.)* *joined Maria and Nancy at Unique Hairstylist on 47 Essex Street, New York, to present a new cabaret performance: (RE) ZONING, MANICURED, a music soiree to describe and denounce the forces of dislocation and dispossession at work in our communities.*

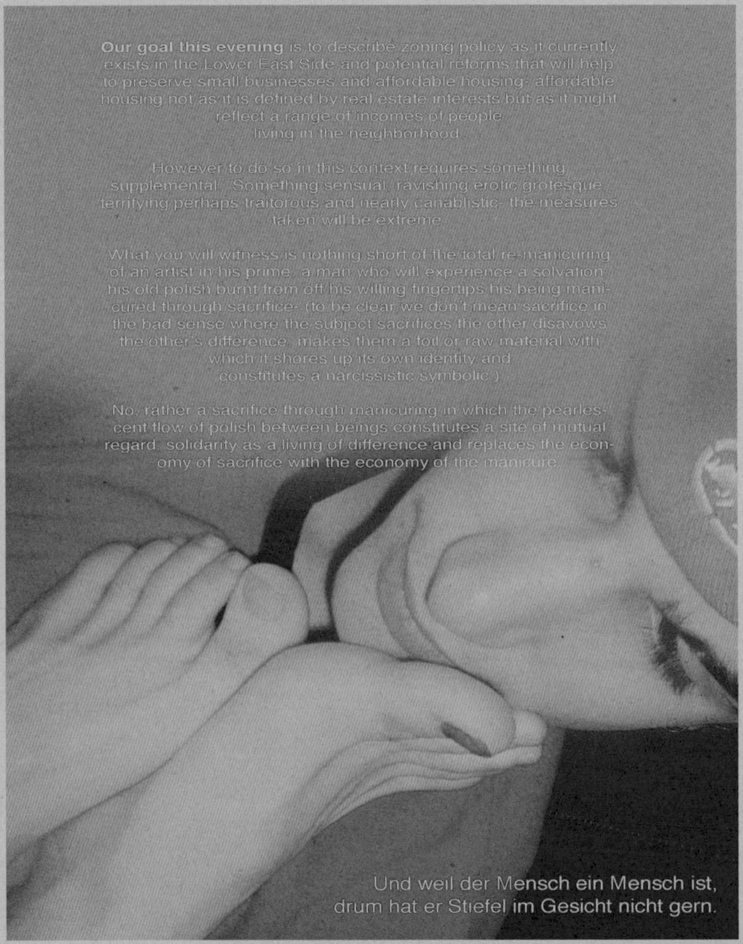

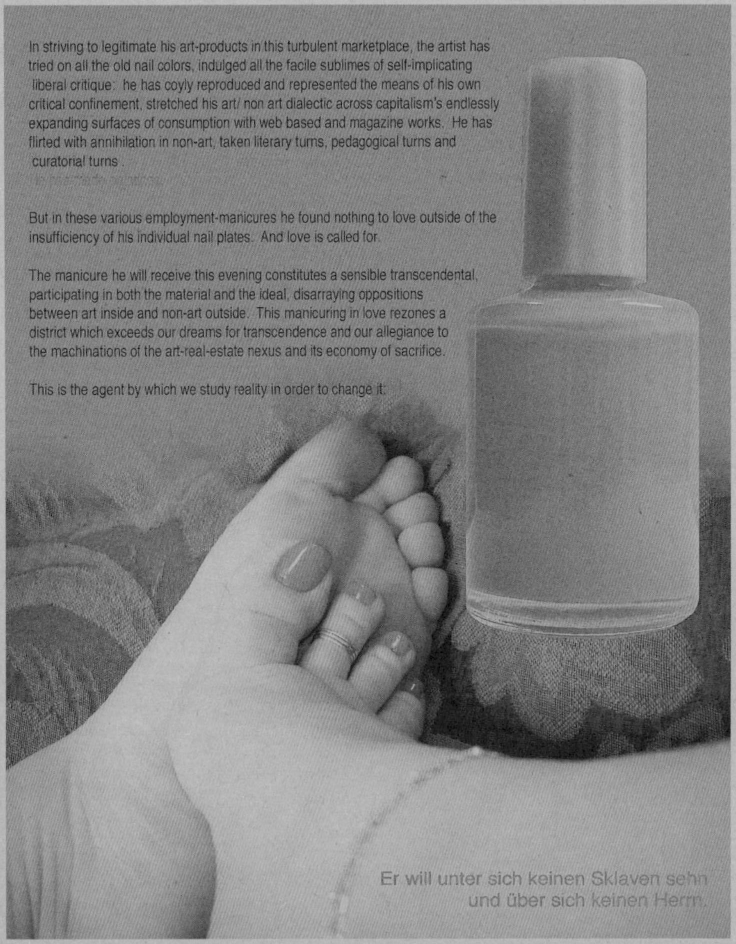

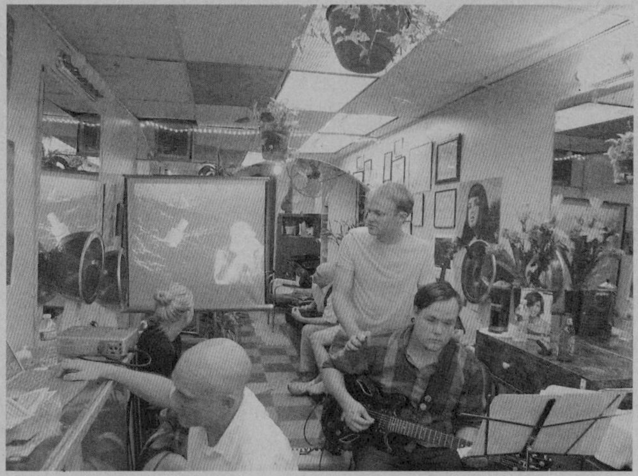

Performance *(re)Zoning Manicured* of H.E.N.S., 2011

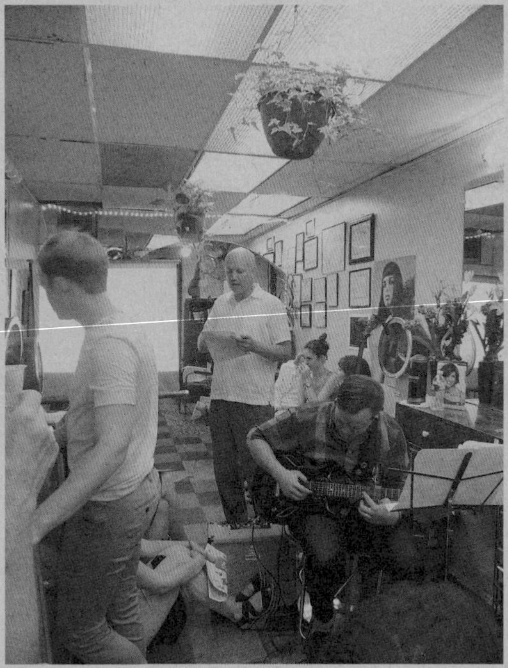

The Hanns Eisler Nail Salon (H.E.N.S.) / Nail Workers Chorus at Unique Hair Stylists, 2011

Zhibin Lin, research coordinator of the Culture and Art Museum of Migrant Workers and Maria, shop owner of the hair salon Unique Hair Stylists, 2011

Ladies and Magentamen, your disco needs you, We must resist the turgid spatial fantasies of capital. We need those of you who are willing to give and receive pedicures in zones of indeterminacy. Come, your nail-plates aglow with non-contractual, insubordinate expenditure for the unfreedom at the heart of love does not belong to contract. Our manicures do not belong to the art-bureaucracy of limits nor to the community betterment plans of capital.

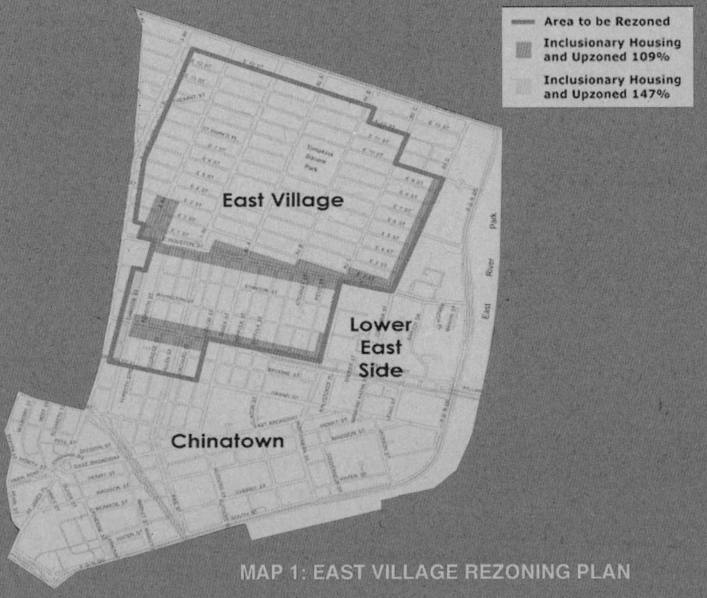

MAP 1: EAST VILLAGE REZONING PLAN

Ludlow 38 is situated in Manhattan's Community District 3, much of which was massively upzoned by the East Village rezoning plan of 2008. This rezoning plan protected the predominantly white and affluent neighborhood to the north of Houston Street from high-rise development by preserving current zoning. The plan even down-zoned in some areas. The area to the south, home to a population that is largely Hispanic and Chinese and with significantly lower median income was not covered by the plan and left open to development. This is part of a long tradition of leaving poor, working class, and ethnically diverse neighborhoods with zoning that allows for extensive new development when luxury desires new territory.

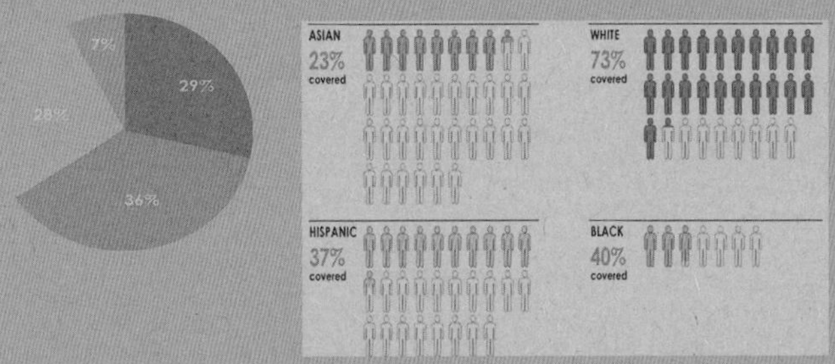

The pie chart shows the breakdown of residents of all of Community District 3 by race. The chart below indicates the percentage of the district's residents protected under the 2008 rezoning plan in relation to race. (based on 2000 census data).

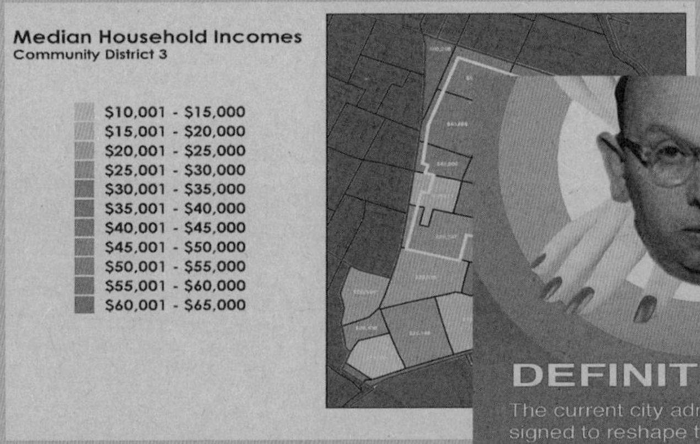

Map showing Median Household Incomes in Community
circled in white represents the area protected by the East

DEFINITIONS

The current city administration is engaged in a long-term program, designed to reshape the city against the class interests of workers. It has rezoned one fifth of the total land in the five boroughs - 6,500 blocks - more than the 6 previous administrations combined. We learn the following definitions in an effort to increase our understanding of the development process and the relations that are thereby produced.

Zoning is a power, held by the state and it's delegates, for instance, city and county governments, to determine by regulation the uses of land.

Floor Area Ratio, or FAR is defined as the gross floor area permitted on a building site divided by the net area of the site, expressed in decimals. FAR is used to regulate the intensity of land use, to manage environmental consequences or to control the mass and scale of development. In New York City, FAR, as a measurement of development potential, has become a valuable commodity. The City estimates that New York city housing authority properties have a combined total of 30.5 million square feet of unused development rights, with 7.6 million square feet in Community District 3 alone.

Upzonig is an increase the permitted density or floor area ratio within a zoning district. Upzoning increases the value of land by increasing the quantity of asset rights on that land.

Affordable Housing refers to dwelling units designated as affordable for the purposes of public subsidy. There are three major housing programs directly financed by the city or state. Between 1990 and 2005 the program lost 22,688 units to privatization, and since 2005 that rate has increased due to the market for rental properties.

APPENDIX / BIOGRAPHIES

HANNS EISLER NAIL SALON / N.W.C. mission is to interrupt the politics of beauty, dislocate the politics of the gallery, and begin to imagine new relations that transform our ways of being in the neighborhood and being in the world; to manicure the ready-to-hand. Our namesake, exile composer Hanns Eisler (1898–1962), was twice robbed of his community; fleeing the rise of fascism in Germany, he found a home in the United States only to find himself on the Hollywood Blacklist, called before HUAC and deported. Like the current denizens of the Lower East Side, power came to deny him community by a vicious process of reorganization, redefinition and rezoning. Eisler wrote some of the most potent hymns to workers rights. We strive to invest his political and artistic project with a lived experience of difference worthy of the contemporary beauty industry; to give an old Marxist a new manicure.

IMMANUEL NESS is professor of political science at Brooklyn College, City University of New York. His work focuses on workers and capitalist political economy, migration and revolutionary movements, labor militancy, and migrant worker activism. He has written numerous essays and books on labor migration, including Immigrants, Unions, and the U.S. Labor Market (Temple University Press, 2005). He is editor of the quarterly, Working USA: The Journal of Labor and Society.

JEFFREY BECKER, International Labor Rights Forum (ILRF) ILRF is an advocacy organization dedicated to achieving just and humane treatment for workers worldwide. ILRF's work supports international labor rights as defined by the International Labor Organization, including the right to freedom of association and collective bargaining, the prohibition of discrimination against women, and the elimination of forced labor and child labor. ILRF promotes decent work around the world. Jeffrey Becker joined ILRF in the summer of 2010, and serves as the program officer for the organization's work in China.

DR. ZHIBIN LIN is the research coordinator of Migrant Workers' Home, a NGO in Beijing, and is part of the Culture and Art Museum of Migrant Workers. Zhibin Lin has taught development sociology, and Gender and Rural Development in China Agricultural University from 1990 to 2001. Since 2003 she is a NGO staff working at migrant workers communities while conducting research in different parts of China. Her research reports include: *Migrant Workers Residential Rights and Future Development* (2009), *Action Research on Migrant Children's Education and Development Projects* (Issue I in 2009, Issue II in 2010), *Where to Go?—Migrant Workers in between the City and the Countryside* (2011).

ELLEN DAVID FRIEDMAN has been a union organizer in Vermont for thirty years, twenty of which she served as the Vermont affiliate of the National Education Association. She was a founder and long-time leader of the Vermont Workers Center and the Vermont Progressive Party, and is a member of the Labor Notes Policy Committee. Since 2006 she has taught labor studies one term per year at Sun Yat-sen University in Guangzhou and has worked at different levels of the labor movement, including grass-roots labor NGOs, the All-China Federation of Trade Unions and with laborscholars.

CARRIE GLEASON is the director of the RETAIL ACTION PROJECT (RAP), a growing network of New York City retail and fashion workers. RAP is dedicated to winning economic justice for retail workers through strategic organizing, policy and research, creative communications, and services. RAP has integrated art into organizing by using video, design and performance to spotlight retail workers' experiences and hold retailers accountable for workplace injustices.

NOT AN ALTERNATIVE is a non-profit organization 501(c)(3) with a mission to affect popular understandings of events, symbols, and history. We curate and produce work that questions and leverages the tools of advertising, architecture, exhibit design, branding, and public relations. Programs are hosted at a variety of venues, including our Brooklyn-based gallery No-Space (formerly known as The Change You Want to See Gallery). Not An Alternative has exhibited work in New York at Eyebeam, Pratt Institute, White Box, NYU, Conflux Festival, New York Art and Book Fair as well as internationally.

MARTY KIRCHNER is an artist and labor organizer based in New York City. He completed the Whitney Independent Study Program in 2010, after graduating from HfBK Städelschule Frankfurt/M in 2009, and the University of California Los Angeles in 2004. A member of the Industrial Workers of the World labor union, he is currently an organizer with Focus on the Food Chain, a campaign to improve conditions of immigrants workers in New York's food processing and distribution warehouses.

AMRAN FREY is an art enthusiast and law student at Humboldt University and Columbia Law School. He assisted in curatorial matters at art spaces in Cairo and New York, and regularly volunteers as a legal advisor to art projects. As an intern at Ludlow 38 he co-organized the side-program to the *The Making of the Chinese New Working Class* exhibition. Having a special interest in non-Western legal cultures his essay *Confucianomics* tries to explain the role of Confucian ideas in the development of the rule of law in China, and how their impact influences the enforcement of Chinese labor law today.

TOBI MAIER is a critic and curator based in New York. From 2006 until 2008 he served as curator at the Frankfurter Kunstverein and also collaborated on Manifesta 7 (Rovereto, Italy) as curatorial adviser. Between 2008 and 2011 he was a curator at Ludlow 38, the downtown satellite space for contemporary art of Goethe-Institut on New York's Lower East Side. He is associate curator for the 30a Bienal de São Paulo, 2012.

MONA WISCHHOFF worked in an advertising agency and studied Economics at University of Cologne. Since 2009 she studies Cultural Studies and Economics at Leuphana University, Lueneburg. Her major fields of interest are communication of contemporary art and sociology of art. Before she started working with Tobi Maier at Ludlow 38 she completed an internship at the foundation and non-commercial art gallery Kunstverein & Stiftung Springhornhof in Neuenkirchen near Hamburg.